PROFILES, POEMS, PRAYERS

CELEBRATING "ORDINARY" PEOPLE

By Danny A. Belrose, D.Min.

Isaac's Press
Blue Springs, Missouri
www.isaacspress.com

Profiles, Poems, Prayers
Celebrating "Ordinary" People

Copyright © 2018 by Danny A. Belrose, Th.M., D.Min.

Isaac's Press
Blue Springs, Missouri
www.isaacspress.com

ISBN 978-0-9844815-4-5

Library of Congress Control Number: 2018957775
Library of Congress subject headings:
Religion & Philosophy
Theology
Christianity
Poetry
Prayer

Cover portraits: Hayden Paul-Adler DeBelleval
                         W. Grant McMurry
                         Barbara Hiles Mesle
Cover design: Danny A. Belrose
Pencil portraits: Danny A. Belrose

Acknowledgments

**I am grateful for everyone who agreed to be profiled
in this collection of poems, prayers
and theological reflections.
Their inclusion does not signify their agreement
with the theological views expressed.**

Everyone featured in this work granted permission for publication (including parental consent for children).

My thanks to Richard and Barbara Howard for reviewing my prose and poetry and for author Richard Brown's advice and assistance in making this work available. I am indebted to Lee Hammond, who opened a new world of artistic expression for me. Lee is an excellent art instructor, encourager, and mentor whose classes and books resurrected an abandoned hobby, improving it beyond measure.

Limiting the scope of this work was difficult; I am blessed with many friends whose stories and contributions to life are worthy of recognition and thanksgiving. Artist and friend, Gary McDonald, emphasizes that the hardest lesson for artists to learn is when to put their brushes down. Guilty as charged. My penchant to revise sections, add profiles, and reflections called for repeated editorial review.

Cheryll Peterman, who skillfully edited my first two books, *Let the Spirit Breathe* and *Wave Offerings,* edited the initial draft of this work, followed by Eileen Terrill, and my wife Penelope. Special thanks to Greg Clark, Herald House and Corporate Communications Editor, whose editing and recommendations greatly improved the final draft. Following Greg's editing, reformatting the manuscript for publication called for additional revisions. Any resulting typos and grammatical errors are mine.

Abundant living invites us to pursue paths of right relationships where hands of friendship and community extend to everyone seeking life's highest good. It begins with re-discovering the extraordinary within the ordinary. It's a journey of justice not judgment. Its ethic is love not law. Its mandate is the worth of all souls, the wonder of creation, and the pervasiveness of life. Living abundantly is a journey of transformation where new horizons beckon and new understandings are birthed. It is not a singular path. For Christians, it is a journey committed to One who set at liberty the bruised and broken-hearted. For non-Christians, it's a path pursuing God's many names, many faces, and sacred rituals that awaken mutual wholeness. For the non-religious, it is a path of secular commitment to love, equity, and collective fairness. Life well lived is life lived authentically in the "here and now," where joy, hope, love, and peace are not perfumed phrases but living words animated by who you are and strive to be.—Danny A. Belrose

Dedication

Beth Ann (Belrose) Morden
February 9, 1962, May 7, 2017

Shock. Denial. Pain. Anger!
Where is God when it's raining?
The shadow-side of *"could have been,*
should have been"—rising, falling,
seeking solace in songs unsung no longer heard or whispered.
A million heartbeats hushed. Death at a distance. No sweet goodbyes.
No warm embrace. No starry home nor heavenly landlord calling. We are
now her home, her rest, her love, her whispered voice, her presence poured in
memory's tears and wounded laughter. Faith's fleeting hope stirs dormant
dreams awake—that mystical, resurrection morn when sleeping souls arise
and cast death's somber shroud aside.
Daughter, sister, wife, mother, grandmother, faithful friend.
Gone before your time, Beth Ann
—your love will never let me go.

When Midnight Comes at Noon

What does one do when midnight comes at noon?
When life imbued with promised years is swept away so soon.
A voice so swiftly silenced.
No passing words, no sweet goodbyes,
    sliced mute by senseless circumstance
    and we who shared her living go on in stunned reprise
    cast deep in death's dark shadow despite a sunlit sky.
"Where, O, death is thy sting?"
It is here. Now. Real. Undeniable.
Painful, poignant, deep, disturbing and personal.
There are no soft farewells.
Grief is love's invoice—signed, sealed and delivered
    by years of summer children, young romance,
    family ties, countless conversations,
    episodes and anecdotes compressed, assessed,
    and lived again in stories sung and told.

Each life is a living letter filled with flaws and failings,
    with hurts and helps and hopes,
    with laughter, tears, and promises spilling on each page.
Line upon line, her letter weaves its way into the fabric of our lives
    shaping who we are and who we may become.
Stopped mid-sentence, her verse lives beyond its writing
    by we who mourn her passing:
    through memories close as yesterday,
    through narratives of love.

She lives within our hearts and minds.
She wanders through our days and nights.
She dwells not in the void of space or in some plot of ground.
She lives in God's abiding grace
    where love and life abound.
Take heart. Sorrow's reign shall end.
Life will shine again.
When midnight comes at noon,
    we need not shape hope's dreams,
    paint its pearly gates, nor weave its feathered wings
    —we need only, trust its flight.

Contents

Introduction

So-Called "Ordinary" People

"It is a serious thing to live in a society of possible gods and goddesses, to remember that the dullest and most uninteresting person you talk to may one day be a creature which, if you saw it now, you would be strongly tempted to worship, or else a horror and a corruption such as you now meet, if at all, only in a nightmare. *All day long we are, in some degree, helping each other to one or other of these destinations. There are no ordinary people.* You have never talked to a mere mortal. Nations, cultures, arts, civilizations—these are mortal, and their lives are to ours as the life of a gnat. But it is immortals whom we joke with, work with, marry, snub and exploit—immortal horrors or everlasting splendors . . . Next to the blessed sacrament itself, your neighbor is the holiest object presented to your senses."—C. S. Lewis: *The Weight of Glory*, adapted [1]

Profiles, Poems, Prayers is a collection of theological reflections inspired by so-called ordinary people whose circle of celebrity is family, friends, and their community. In a sense, this is a book about you and me. Your portrait and name may not grace its pages, but you will find yourself here and there in the prayers offered and the people profiled. They represent the giggling toddler skipping down your street, your work colleague, your favorite aunt, teacher, coach, or workout instructor—names and faces of everyday folk— who may never gain fame or fortune but are anything but ordinary.

Theologian Walter Brueggemann says we are living in "a prose flattened world.[2] We certainly live in a world, where the word *ordinary* wounds wonder. The term "ordinary people" undermines individuality and diversity. With many people profiled here, you'd be hard-pressed to see them as "ordinary" on any level. Some have so many accolades, achievements, degrees, and notoriety that they can't possibly be viewed as "everyday folk." Conversely, kings, queens, actors, singers, high-achievers are "everyday folk" whose circumstance, talent, hard-work, and good fortune have awarded them celebrity status. We need to discover the extraordinary within the ordinary—the hidden depths of others, including those most close to us.

When we awaken to the inestimable worth of family, friend, workmate, and stranger, we rediscover wonder. We tend to gulp life. We need to sip and savor its wonder and see every person as an unrepeated miracle of creation. Life's splendor is shrouded by *everydayness*—the tendency to live life by default. Today repeats yesterday. Tomorrow replicates today. Day in and day out, we sleep-walk through mind-numbing routines oblivious to new discoveries and life's blessings. The school bus driver, the cop on the beat, the lady behind the pharmacy counter, and the teen bagging groceries become background players milling about off stage. We praise actors, athletes, and celebrities while our next-door neighbor—who may never grace a headline— contributes to our welfare daily.

What is extraordinary about a two-year-old playing with Mr. Potato Head, an infant attempting to stand, a teacher, a preacher, a mother, a father, a couple of boys playing in the sand? Nothing and perhaps everything! A contradiction in terms? No more so than a recent TV commercial's bizarre disclaimer, "Real People! Not actors!" *Profiles, Poems, Prayers* echoes Lewis's proclamation: "*Next to the blessed sacrament itself, your neighbor is the holiest object presented to your senses.*" Lewis invites us to discover the extraordinary in *so-called ordinary people* and to consider our unique contribution to others.[3]

Theological Filters

This is not a "believe-what-I-believe" book! My theological reflections have no agenda other than to candidly share my on-going exploration with "life's deeper reality." Someone said theologians keep talking because they are afraid someone will believe their last sentence. I believe we must keep talking, listening, probing, pondering, and stretching for our best understanding of life's mysteries and what we may (or may not) ascribe as the Divine. Life's journey is crammed with ambiguity—a mysterious flux of joy, hope, love, pain, suffering and healing. Not to probe such ambiguity deeply or even in passing is impossible. Lack of inquiry (theological and otherwise) mitigates our basic nature. We are creatures of curiosity forever pondering: "Who?" "What?" "When?" "Where?" "Why and How?"

Ironically, some Christians dismiss supernatural aspects of other world religions as nonsense while accepting without question Christianity's mystical elements. It's an "our metaphysics trumps your metaphysics" polemic. The *why and how of my faith* concludes that Christianity does not have an exclusive claim to truth. Said another way, God is not a Christian. My reflections are therefore *open-ended* musings for believers, skeptics, agnostics, atheists, and humanists who may question the divinity of Jesus but who subscribe to his compassionate ministry and message.[4]

Christianity must jettison redemptive exclusivity and embrace the many names and faces of God revered in all religions that affirm life, equality, justice and love. It must affirm those whose time, talent, and treasure contribute to the welfare of others, but who are not committed to religiosity or belief in God. It is not what religious or ideological banner we wave or what we claim to believe. The ultimate value of theology and ideology is determined by kindness. Belief systems are measured by how we live in relationship with others and our environment. This does not mean beliefs do not matter. What we believe is important recognizing that at our best, we only approximate the truth.

Poet Robert Frost's headstone reads, "I have had a lover's quarrel with the world." I've had a lover's quarrel with my faith. The most committed believer dances between assurance and doubt. The opposite of faith is not doubt; the opposite of faith is fear. Theology is poetry and metaphor—a fumbling attempt to capture in words our best understanding (or negation) of the mystery we call God. Theology is inescapably subjective. I have learned to say, "It seems to me" rather than "That's the way it is!" The foundation of my faith as recorded in *Let the Spirit Breathe* remains unchanged.

There are serendipitous moments when *the Presence* breaks in, breathes on me, and takes my breath away. Suddenly, philosophy and theology vanish. All my lofty perceptions and mental constructs are stripped away. For one brief shining moment, I have a lively awareness of an inexpressible essence of divine love. This—and this alone—is ultimately all that really matters. All credos, programs, and formulas, fade in this moment of pervasive enlightenment that is at once cognitively and emotively transfixed. It is an "aha," an irrefutable acquisition of what is intuitively known, yet seldom fully appropriated: At the very core of creation, everything comes down to love.[5]

Word-portraits of Jesus are always wanting. From time to time, my verbal brush strokes are abstract and undefined. The point is, I keep painting, revising fixed outlines, removing muddy tones and hues, and sometimes restoring images long ago abandoned. A question posed in a recent Volkswagen TV commercial equally applies to my attempts to accurately portray Jesus. Seated around a meeting table where a CEO unleashes a barrage of doom and gloom business results to his management team, one listener pipes up and says, "*You know what this room needs? It needs a smile!*" My prayers, and reflections may at times sound a sour note affronting traditionally held beliefs. If that is your experience, take a deep breath, *smile*, and read on. Theology is guesswork! It's both a head and heart game. Hopefully such musings will open doors for on-going self-dialogue, permitting you to shout anew a resounding "YES" to life, as together we ponder the strange, inexplicable stirrings of Love's Spirit that will not let us go. Here then, are the theological brush strokes that color my writing.

I am a *liberal, conservative, agnostic, mystic,* Christian. I explore progressive theological perspectives. I hold fast to moral convictions that call me to "do justice, love kindness, and walk humbly with your God" (Micah 6:8). My Christian agnosticism is not a contradiction in terms. "All intelligent faith in God" said Harry Emerson Fosdick, "has behind it a background of humble agnosticism.[6] Certitude is theology's nemeses. "God is a thought," said Joseph Campbell, "God is an idea, but its reference is to something that transcends all thinking."[7] Agnosticism is uncertainty—a healthy skepticism that serves to remind me *I am smart enough to know I am not smart enough.* I have experienced *mystical happenings* academia and logic cannot explain. I respect and learn from others whose religious beliefs are different from mine. Frederick Buechner's eloquent confession of faith best describes my emerging theology:

I believe without the miracles I have prayed for then; that is what I am explaining. I believe because certain uncertain things have happened, dim half-miracles, sermons and silences and what not. Perhaps it is my believing itself that is the miracle I believe by. Perhaps it is the miracle of my own life: that I, who might so easily not have been, am; who might so easily at any moment, even now, give the whole thing up, nonetheless by God's grace do not give it up and am not given up by it[8]

Poems or Prayers?

I am hard-pressed to differentiate poetry from prayer. I pray at my keyboard. Not *"Dear God"* prayers. Not petitions. Not journaling, *per se*. Not *"Let's see if I can write a poem or some mind-blowing prose."* I may begin with a phrase having no destination in mind. Sometimes it goes nowhere. Sometimes it does. But even when it is gibberish, *it is prayer*—a time when I am accessible to the unexpected—a time when I awaken to life's beauty and mysterious sustaining source. In a sense, every sentence, regardless of literary worth, ends with an untyped "Amen." I am pleased if a turn of phrase speaks to me, however, the value of my keyboard prayers is not cleverness or composition; it is measured by my responsiveness to *life's deeper reality— what* C. S. Lewis called, "Surprised by Joy," and the source of that joy.[9]

No Book is Original

Books are no more than a writer's personal musings informed, enriched and influenced by others. Each scratch of pen on paper, each click of a keyboard is indebted to a host of witnesses present and past whose wisdom has preceded it. *Profiles, Poems, Prayers* is a bouquet crammed with the colorful insights of others wrapped in my ribbon of words. I have credited sources while not always cognizant what is mine and what unconsciously is borrowed. Whose voice have I failed to honor? Whose thoughts, phrases, and ideas have slipped through not attributed? Hopefully, few.

I hope this book will encourage you to vicariously discover what I discovered writing it: surprising discoveries about friends you think you know; a renewed appreciation for diversity; affirmation that life—in all its expressions —is co-dependent and sacred; and a renewed appreciation for those who enrich your life in simple yet profound ways. May you enjoy reading this collection of profiles and prayers as much as I did writing it. You know whose portraits, profiles and praise you would include were this your book. These are but a few of mine.

Love Without Limits
Richard and Barbara Howard

Do nothing from selfish ambition or conceit, but in humility regard others as better than yourselves. Let each of you look not to your own interests, but to the interests of others. —Philippians 2: 3–4 NRSV

Choosing a title for Dick and Barbara's portrait was challenging. *"Faithful Companions,"* and *"Blessed to Be a Blessing,"* describe this dedicated couple whose gifts and graces bless stranger and friend alike.

For twenty-nine years Dick served as Community of Christ's historian. His uncanny ability to rehearse dates, times, places, names of who was where, when, and why, of obscure historical events is mind-boggling. He is the youngest octogenarian I know. His insights and clever observations are sprinkled with wit and wisdom. An accomplished "Mr. Fixit," Dick suffers from a severe case of "Yes-itis." Whether caught up in a personal project or having just put his feet up to watch a baseball game, Dick responds immediately to assist those in need. "I'm sorry I can't help" is not in his lexicon.

Barbara worked for twenty-eight years for *Herald Publishing* House copyediting her church's *Restoration Witness* and monthly *Saint's Herald* magazine. Reading is not a pastime for Barbara; it is prime time! She insatiably consumes books and can recite verbatim quotations from numerous favorite authors.

Barbara's effusiveness is unparalleled. The phrase "All emphasis is no emphasis" has no meaning for her. Everything from a bumblebee to a Broadway show is "fantastic, wonderful, the best!" Everyone is the most brilliant, most beautiful, most gifted, most intelligent, kind, considerate, skilled, and talented person she has ever met. Her daily litany of the words best, amazing, greatest, superb, terrific, outstanding, incredible has worn them so thin mere mortals may soon be unable to use them. Her accolades are unabated. She absolutely means what she says because for Barbara, everything *is* new. "Gratitude" is her middle name (perhaps, her first)! Regardless of sunshine or shadow, she believes tomorrow is always better than yesterday. It's a positive mental disorder more of us should have!

Dick and Barbara have written several books, papers, articles, and hymn texts and have conducted seminars on a wide range of topics. Their courage to challenge historical and theological myths have not been without cost. Despite criticism from disgruntled, conservative church members, Barb and Dick have remained faithful to their church. Had such rejection been directed at me and mine I would have been numbered among the church alumni. They championed women's ordination, "open Communion" (Eucharist for nonmembers) and LGBTQ rights decades before official church acceptance. Dick and Barbara defy the label "ordinary."

Wrinkled Reminders

Touching but seldom touched they lie now in her lap,
tired and inert—wrinkled reminders of giving and receiving.
Years of holding on and letting go.
Bless the work of these hands, O God,
these hands that have helped, and held, and healed,
that have cooked, and ironed, and wiped back tears,
sewn on buttons and straightened ties.
Bless the work of these hands.

Now Is Forever[10]

Dimpled hands, pudgy feet, tiny toes, and chubby cheeks. Weathered hands, wrinkled face, wispy hair, and aching feet. Decades pass, and nothing lasts. We laugh. We weep. We give and take. We dance. We mourn. We love and hate and long to live forever, God. Forever? We long to live forever yet fail to live today. Eternity is tucked away in every breath of life. Savor it with all you have and are. For "now" is forever—the season's constant sway. Yesterday has slipped away—tomorrow never comes. Its promise is a hope away but "now" is here to stay. Wait no more. Debate no more. Live fully every day!

Winter Hope

Withered winter trees stripped of leaves and color, standing, waiting, antici-
pating spring, wondering if there's something now—some task worthwhile,
some service seen, the hope of being needed here and now, not merely filling
time and space in this cold place—alone, forlorn, forgotten. Fringed in
white, they stand apart, their naked arms not touching, so unaware, their
beauty here no artist's brush or poet's pen can capture their abiding. And we,
O God, stripped winter bare, whose seasons are declining, whose gifts of
spring no longer sing youth's tireless songs reciting, cannot stand with empty
hands or put to rest our dreaming. Nor can we wait or hesitate to give from
our receiving, for winter's every season now—our time for hope's redeeming.

Little Sacraments

The little sacraments between us. Serendipitous drops of living water that
quench the soul's drought. Like pearly beads of hope, they slip, and slide and
seep inside, seldom seen or realized until they slake our sacred thirst denied
by everydayness. They find the cracks within our souls. They pour their light
inside, reminding us that we are one with all that is, with all that's been, for
stardust shapes our living. Little sacraments—the holy unction of
acceptance. Secrets said and shared, the bread and wine of friendship, a
starling's song, a starlit night, twilight's kiss, a newborn's cry, a flamed-
tinged sky—all these and MORE. These little sacraments between us,
stripped of rite and ritual—a touch, a look, a word of hope—drops of living
water given and received. Drink deeply.

Rhythms Undecided

Wisdom sings its own sweet song and dances in the shadows.
Each pirouette a step of grace explored,
    pursuing words that free one's heart and mind
    and breaks hope's chains confining.
"Awake! Awake!" creation cries, "there is no us, there is no them,
    for I am you and you are me and we are ONE, not more!
Lift your eyes from off the page.
Soar above the score. Play your music. Dance your dance.
Wisdom wrapped in holy writ is metaphor and mystery.
Its music calls for all to dance in rhythms undecided
    —where every soul shares equal worth, and Love is undivided.

Price Tags

IT ISN'T FAIR, God! She can't act, sing or dance—she's famous for being famous. They who report the news have become the news. We're drunk on celebrity—a culture of no-names pinning vicarious hopes on any name, fleetingly aglow in fame's fickle strobe. On again. Off again. Millions paid to throw and catch a ball. Gleaming white teeth, hair with highlights, a figure to die for, an actor to tell me what gum to chew. It's senseless, God!
We celebrate counter-culture heavies "rapping" their way to the bank, while in a cardboard tenement, a mother struggles to keep her baby warm. Who mixed the price tags? Billions spent to keep gun barrels hot, terrorists at bay, nations on edge, innocent children short-changed as collateral damage. All for safety and freedom? Meanwhile, TV preachers scream God's prosperity's game—funds and fame awaiting—while prayers ascend to Jesus, Allah, Krishna, Mary. Each faithful soul stretching hope beyond reason that peace may abide, the price tags adjusted, and life's pie justly shared.

> *We know what we want but not what we need.*
> *Give us what we need, God. Give us peace.*
> *Peace at war with conflict.*
> *Peace that refuses to accept the unacceptable.*
> *Peace that equates all life as celebrity,*
>   *where every soul's price tag is valued,*
>   *in or out of the spotlight.*

Reflection: Second Childhood

Why not a third, fourth, persistent childhood—where years are neither measured nor assumed? A seventy-year-old giggle. A ninety-year-old break dance? (Well, maybe not). The absolute abandonment of "having it all together"—the refusal to abandon "WOW!" A middle-age euphoric discovery? Middle age? Now there's a concept. Middle of what? Isn't any age, 'middle age'—the delight of being between what 'has been,' 'what is,' and 'what may be,' good, bad, or indifferent? Second childhood second thoughts: Face it, childhood has its shadow-side—"the ME-MINE-CENTER OF ATTENTION-THE WORLD IS HERE TO SERVE ME-CRY UNTIL I GET MY WAY" psychosis. Life's joy at any age is really a matter of 'letting go' and 'holding on." Letting go of 'self-inflation." Letting go of "the too muchness" and "too littleness" of self and holding on tightly to what truly matters: love, liberty, the lively notes of caring, kindness, compassion, and community played minute by minute by creation's glorious symphony. To seek beauty and live it.

Freedom of Speech
Evelyn Winter DeBelleval

Two-year-old Evelyn DeBelleval gives *Mr. Potato Head* his mouth and grants him *freedom of speech.*[11] She knows mouths are very, very important. Mouths are for eating yummy things, yellow things, orange things, red things, broccoli, beans, and things seldom seen. Mouths are for growing tiny teeth, learning how to use a toothbrush, tasting ice cream, drinking chocolate milk, giggling, and saying silly things. Mouths are for kissing and hissing, and *sometimes* for spitting. Mouths are for tasting snowflakes, eating peanut butter, smiling at jokes, and crying for hurts. Mouths are for saying, "I LOVE you!" "Let's share!" "That's bad!" "I'm sorry. You're sad." Mouths are for lots and lots of things—did I mention ice cream?

Mr. Potato Head Gets a Mouth

"Mr. Potato" can see north and south,
    roll his round eyes and frown with a pout,
    but he can't say a sound till she plugs in his mouth.
He can't giggle or laugh or stick out his tongue,
    make silly sounds or sing funny songs!
She selected his eyes, the shape of his nose.
He has ONLY a head—no body, no toes,
    so, she gave him BIG ears to make up for those.
And last but not least, she plugged in red lips
    for eating and smiling and sharing bright tips:
    like oranges are orange, apples are red,
    mosquito bites sting and itch while in bed,
    birds can sing songs without using words,
    and mouths that are mad say words that are bad,
    so, never be mean or tears will be seen.
A mouth is for smiling and saying, "hello,"
    for making new friends, not just friends you know,
    no matter their color, whether tall, thin, or stout.
A smile is a smile; it's NEVER a pout.
And then with a grin he looked up her way,
"Everyone's welcome to share and to play. Let's laugh and be happy!
Let's have a fun day!" And these were the first words she heard him to say!

Violated

Simplicity, complexity, duplicity, and irony dance together
    and we're not quite sure who's leading and who's following.
Whatever language we employ, we're bound to step on toes.
When words become weapons, everyone suffers.
Abuse diminishes both speaker and listener
    —BOTH are wounded, and community dies.
Whenever a race or a face, millionaire or mendicant,
    someone, tall, short, fat or thin is put down,
    everyone is put down. Indignity begs no allegiance;
    it discredits giver and receiver.
The righteousness in which we are self-wrapped
    is wafer thin, crushed easily by a word or deed.
Blatant or benign, wherever hatred raises its head
    dissing race, religion, height, weight, dress size,
    gender, or orientation. Everyone is violated.

God was a woman some 30,000 years before God became male. She gave birth, sprinkled rain on parched soil, shined her sunlight by day and moonlight by night. She whispered winds, shouted storms, painted skies pink, signed her name with lightning. "Sophia" made each morning! She was good and sometimes not so good. Just like every god.[12]

Sophia Makes a Morning

She slept in. Missed her first sunrise.
After all, it was hers, wasn't it? And it was good.
  "It was good, wasn't it?" she pondered as she swept her
    sheets aside, yawned deeply, rubbed her eyes
    and drank in the wonder of this natal "Sabbath" morn.
"SABBATH!" Yes, "Sabbath, that's a good name."
She said it softly, slowly watching each letter spring to life.
"Patience, patience, dear day of rest, some will find you,
    drink you in, stop their silly song
    and let the music of the soul soothe their ragged week."
And it will be good. So, good.
Her hair a mess, her hands star-touched and burning,
    red, raw, bruised and bleeding.
A cosmos in the making, ever-changing, for it was IN her,
OF her, THROUGH her, so much more than the sum
    of its parts: a hurling, whirling ecstasy ever pregnant,
    living, dying, stretching, sighing.
CREATION. Unrestrained, spilling through the ink of space,
    birthing new realities—a never ending panoply
    where hope and possibility escape the sludge
    of "it can't be done" and leave the rules behind.
"So, exciting," she mused.
"Above, beneath, around, within—it is me and I am it!"
Breakfast could wait. She took her time,
    your time, my time, all time, for time had not begun.
Stepping into her slippers she looked out her window,
    rubbed a smudge or two away and gazed
    at all she had done, all she was doing,
    all she was, is, and would be.
A tear coursed down her cheek.
She choked, smiled, could barely get the words out,
    "It really is good, isn't it!"

Word Magic

She came on like a tank, God,
bullets blazing, blue haze raising,
each word hitting its mark, dead on.
And me? I am silent, God.
Red cape tattered. The "S" on my chest riddled and ripped.
"Freedom of speech," you say. "Turn the other cheek," you say,
Easy for you to say, you're not on the receiving end!
You're sound asleep in that onion-skinned book.
Well, I have onionskin too, God, and I'm bleeding inside!
Nevertheless, I'm playing my part.
Coat-hanger smile, wide as a mile.
Nodding my head, eyes straight ahead.
Making it. Taking it. Faking it.
Playing Jesus. Holding my tongue.
Nailed to the cross with each word she says.
Not a whimper, a whine, a tear, or a sigh,
swallowing my anger, boiling inside!
It's all just "word magic" isn't it?
Bane or blessing. Damage or delight.
Just sharing what's inside.
But it's more, than inside, isn't it?

It's outside, landing somewhere, taking up residence,
building, breaking, blessing or cursing.
Sharp, snappy sentences short on meaning, long on feeling,
casting their spell—understood and misunderstood
hitting a million hearts and minds dead on!
"Let there be light" and there was light.
Easy for you to say! Let there be kindness. Let there be forgiveness.
Let there be tolerance, acceptance, wholeness, and peace.
Let there be love! And there was, and we saw it was good!

Every Word We Speak

Forgive, our racial slurs, God, our camps of segregation,
for we have let our words be god and suffered separation.
Strip hate from all we say. Let the words we speak today
bless each soul that comes our way in our giving and receiving.

Small Talk

Words, words, words. Millions of words.
Pundits, newsprint, talk shows. Hi-profile, media-hungry users
      of every stripe and color having their say.
The pure and impure weighing in on faddish debates.
Facebook, Instagram, LinkedIn, linked out!
What we say is wed to what we do.
Jesus was one with his word; he lived what he said.
Raise up each nation, defeat discrimination,
      erase humiliation! It's not a matter of being politically correct.
It's knowing I am you and you are me and living that integrity.

Clergy Confession . . .

We confess the slow re-birthing of our lives
      when the windows of our souls remained closed
      to the fresh breath of your Spirit, God.
We confess our functional atheism
      —those rare but telling moments when church
      eclipsed family, and programs replaced people.
We confess our propensity to place prophetic leadership
      beyond the pale of human frailty.
We confess our failure to hear the silent cries of those
      who bear life's burdens.
We confess our complicity of silence—the muting of what we have learned
      hidden by homilies that please and protect.
We confess our protracted self-sufficiency
      —our stillborn prayer life, discipleship's thin veneer
      stripped bare by anger's wounding words.
We confess the power of your Spirit
      to sweep from our lives ashes of discontent.
We confess your joy, your hope, your peace, your forgiveness
      —that abiding grace that reminds us, amid the dark night of the soul,
      faith is not rooted in programs, polity, people or creedal proclamations,
      but in One who stretched love upon a tree,
      revealed our divinity and called us
      to the right arrangement of relationships
      through which creation is blessed.
We confess tomorrow awaits and we will rise to meet it
      assured you go before us.

Cool Choughts
Tyler William Hoyt

Sometimes a soul needs to waste time—time to unplug, catch a sparkle of sunlight, gaze at a leaf instead of the pavement, hear the cadence of a cricket. Countless voices vie for our attention. Cell phones, texts, tablets, media posts, meetings and mayhem squeeze out the day. Did you see her smiling face? Her eyes? The jogger sprinting past? That amber sky? An infant's toothless grin? The one you love at the breakfast table? Days become reruns. Same players, same plot. Everydayness swallows us and gobbles up tomorrow.

We need to sip life, not gulp it. We need to let today BE today, free of yesterday's bumps, bruises, and tomorrow's concerns. Savor the present. Experience "being" stripped of "doing." Slow down. Take time to "waste time"—to pause, breathe deeply, meditate, and abandon calendars, clocks, and pressing deadlines. Let "now" be pregnant with possibilities and joy!

Six-year-old Tyler William Hoyt's "now" is pregnant. He has one niggling concern. He wants to go home. Mythologist Joseph Campbell said: "All of life is meditation."[13] Tyler is meditating and cogitating. His life is suddenly a bitter, biting breeze, a cold stone perch, and an eternity of waiting for mom, dad, and twin brother Tristan to return. This is not everydayness! "Family Picture Day." A brisk, cool day. And Tyler hates being cold. *Why so many pictures? I know what I look like! I'm cold! I want to go home!*

Cool Thoughts

He sat on a stone cold and alone wishing his parents
    would soon take him home.
The weather was chilly, he thought it so silly
    to shiver and quiver just for a picture
    to smile for a while in an old photo file
    or hang on a wall in somebody's hall.
"LOOK! I'm a TWIN. Take TWO pics of HIM.
We look the same. Just stick on my name,
    and save me from freezing and going insane.
    No one will guess I wasn't there,
    Tristan and I have the same color hair."
I could sit in the car and wait till they're done,
    away from these clouds that are hiding the sun.
I'm not very old. I can't stand the cold.
No teasing. I'm freezing! And soon I'll be sneezing,
I wish they'd be quicker before I get sicker.
They won't come this way; the brush is much thicker.
He then heard a click, a chuckle, and snicker.
Someone snuck up and just took his picture!

Slivers of Reality

What you can't see bears watching! Subtle slivers of reality staring through sad eyes, saying, "Slow down you're shuffling too fast! Sip a little wonder, share a little light, color is around you screaming day and night, 'Wake up, I'm here! You're losing sight.'" Sacred sunsets, candle flames, purple mountains, children's games, inky nights and silhouettes, swirling seas in pirouettes, windswept waves that never wane, a raindrop's dance on window panes. Your day is filled with heaven's flame, unseen, unheard, unnamed. It winks within the shadows—it burns within the night. It blazes in the bright of day—it's somewhere out of sight, somewhere in the rush and go, somewhere not proclaimed—hidden in your busyness, life is whispering your name.

One Primal Truth

Wake-up calls. Unplanned, unstructured, unbidden.
Brief interludes of grace when grayness drains away.
How? When? Where and why? They come.
They go. Seen. Felt. Heard. Serendipitous.
Brief shining moments when little mysteries
*   are unwrapped and wonder comes alive again:*
*   a setting sun, an autumn leaf, summer wind,*
*   the smell of rain, the delicate shape of newborn lips,*
*   dancing wheat and grain.*
A million miles from Sabbath, the sacred becomes mundane,
*   cloaked by self-inflation till awakening comes again*
*   and strips my soul of arrogance and lays my constructs bare.*
Lofty thoughts, learned texts, faith with all its faces, theologies,
*   philosophies stripped clean from my embraces,*
*   no longer dance inside me. All assumed profundities*
*   escape my mind's peripheries. One epiphany. One primal truth remains,*
*   within, without, beneath, above —it all comes down to Love!*

Lost Light

They slip away so quickly. A glimpse of feathered wings, a starling's song, a boiling sunset drowned in sparkling seas. The silent death of crimson skies chasing lost light bruised by brooding night. Wispy clouds sweep the moon aside, while seagulls glide above the deep soon to fade from view. Day is done. Lost. Gone. Night prevails. Words, phrases, the sound of her voice, her smile, the tilt of her head, her touch, embrace, her presence lost to memory's fleeting years. Were her eyes blue? Brown? Her hair grey? What did she say? How did she say it? Can I write it down? Gone. Gone. Countless sunsets set and done. A million mornings mourned and lost—rehearsed, renewed, re-born, dressed now in memory's tattered clothes.

Reflection: Is the Church Willing to Die?

Any institution, religious or otherwise, inordinately focused on its own survival is not primarily focused on its mission. The question is, "Is the Church willing to die in order to be resurrected? Is the Church willing to be radically smaller in number in order to be larger in integrity?" Paradoxically, though this journey may close the door on supernatural theism, rather than shrinking the God we worship, it may indeed expand the wonder of the new God we meet.

Sacrifice
Marjorie Jean Belrose

June, 1947. Marjorie Jean Belrose sits trancelike in a hospital waiting room in the breaking hours of a warm spring morning that will change her life forever. Physicians fight to keep the pending death of her husband at bay, and in the burgeoning bleakness surrounding her, she knows he will not survive. Nevertheless, fear drains from her. She is not alone. In weeks, months, and years to come, the dark night of the soul will frequently overwhelm her, but in the heartbreaking hours of this early morn, it fails to claim her. She experiences an Abiding Presence within and around her. Strangely at peace in the face of unfathomable loss, she foresees herself raising her two boys, assured she will never be alone.

Wrapped in a dreamlike state of denial my mother awakened each morning looking for Easter only to find Good Friday. Time would see her working in a cleaning shop, taking in boarders, cooking breakfasts, rushing off to work, preparing meals in the evening, practicing hymns, doing laundry and ironing for her boys and three boarders in a crowded home. With

25

enduring faith and hard work she overcame whatever challenge confronted her.

Her most pressing desire was to ensure her young sons would not be strangers to the *Abiding Presence* that rested upon her in her most needful hour—a desire that *never* waned. Each evening she practiced hymns for Sunday. We sang together as her weary fingers danced over black-and-white keys, blending their tones into music of joy, hope, and praise. Night after night, while worries and bills lay abandoned on the kitchen table, she took us hand in hand to a small sofa in our living room where we knelt for family prayer. It was there, faith swallowed fear, feelings of inadequacy, and the daily challenge to put bread on our table. It was there, courage defeated demands of tomorrow. It was there, my brother, and I met Jesus.

Birds Sing in the Rain

Suffering sings salvation's song.
None escape its woeful chant. Millionaire, martyr, miscreant,
*   the least, the lost, the labeled—every child is mine.*[14]
I hear each cry. I taste each tear.
I bind each wound with aching time
*   that blunts pain's fire with passing years.*
Birds sing in the rain.
Goodness sings salvation's song;
*   joy smothers hurt, dawn awaits the death of night,*
*   the faintest light dispels the dark.*
Young, old, gay, straight—every child is mine.
I hear each cry. I taste each tear.
I soothe the scars of yesteryear
*   and pour hope's balm on grief and fear.*
LOVE dances on.
Birds sing in the rain.
Each season spills its pain and joy.
Wind, rain, creation's refrain, spinning stars,
*   vibrating strings, a multiverse cacophony*
*   wherein the cosmos sings.*
LOVE shapes and sifts each grain of sand
*   and weeps for songs unsung from muted*
*   souls so sound asleep they fail to understand*
*   that symphonies and ecstasies lie hidden in their hands.*
Birds sing in the rain.
Each day, rain or shine, through tears and laughter
*   she heard them—and so did we.*

Never Defeated

Little things. A widow's tear. Dishpan hands.
Red, wrinkled, worn weary.
Aching gray eyes—gentle, loving, forgiving.
Brown-gravy stew. Buttons sewn. Shoes shined.
Washing. Ironing. Three jobs waiting. Boarders to feed.
Boys to bathe. Hugs. Hymns.
Fingers that fly o'er black and white keys.
A cut. A scrape. A kiss to make them better.
Constantly giving. Never requiring.
Mother, father, worker, worrier.
Alone in the night. Never defeated.

Abiding Presence

The sun sleeps-in this morning.
Fog's gray blanket shrouds life, limb, and soul.
So, little light to guide my way.
Opportunity scratches at new possibilities,
*   new learnings, new hopes for mind, heart, and soul.*
Shadows seek shape and substance.
Silence pounds its fist:"AWAKE! AWAKE!"
The stillborn morn awaits and screams my name.
So much slips away, unheard, unseen:
*   the crunch of grass beneath my feet,*
*   lacework webs spun leaf to leaf,*
*   morning mist upon my cheek,*
*   a brush of breeze, the balm of spring, a symphony of trees.*
And through it all, above it all, beneath, within, behind it all
*   —darkness or light, sunshine or shadow,*
*   One who claims no single name breaks my reverie.*
A fleeting awareness—an "abiding presence,"
*   a deeper reality, nether external nor internal,*
*   but the very essence of "being" comes unbidden:*
*   an acquisition of what I intuitively know*
*   yet seldom appropriate:"the core of creation is love!"*
Grace caresses winter trees,
*   withered grass, and icy seas with warmth and light.*
Love shines its life upon me and stirs my dreams awake.

Hard Day's Night[15]

"Now I lay me down to sleep." I wish!
The older I get, the less I sleep.
Do you have trouble sleeping, God?
Sorry, I forgot; you never sleep. Look, you're missing out.
There's nothing like a warm bed at the end of a hard day.
Don't tell me, you don't have hard days, God,
I know better. I contribute to them.
Hand in hand with millions of others,
*   I make most days a "hard day's night."*
Presidents, kings, dictators, terrorists.
Lives on and off death's victory at the wave of hand?
Stock-market jockeys riding inside information
*   —a take-over here, a bankruptcy there.*
Suicide, genocide, hurricanes, and drought.
No wonder you don't sleep. Somebody must wind the clock
*   keep it running, rain or shine, fair weather or fowl.*
Rest? Relaxation? Downtime, God? You don't have a prayer!
You're too busy! Hoping, wishing, and praying
*   —that WE will awake!*

Paying Attention to Life

Spirituality isn't religion. Spirituality is 'paying attention' to life.
It's waking up to wonder! It's taking life for gratitude instead of for granted!
Sadly, we ignore joy's clock. We fail to see its smiling face or hear its silent
ticking. We think our days are endless days. Until, they're not!

Melody

Let music PLAY! Not its notes and instruments—nor they who pluck and play
them. Let melody take flight beyond pages scored with sprinkling dots high,
low, and blending. Set free its soaring rhythm, each silent staff held fast by
inky dictums—here, then there, evoked by flawless printing. Come, let music
PLAY—freed from wooden fingers enslaved by what is written. Its soul is
more than soft, loud, arpeggios harmony—it lives within creation's song that
births each star, each baby's breath, the silence and the keeping. And God is
caught in dogma's web, in holy writ, in songs of praise whose measured
strands of good and ill, of do's and don'ts, and worship's dance are snuggly
fit by far-fetched faith—reduced by our poor spelling.

Unfinished
Burton (Curly) Belrose

I started this sketch of my father, Burton Alexander (Curly) Belrose, several years ago but have been unable to complete it. I draw from photos and though I have finalized portraits of people I've never met, it is infinitely easier to capture the essence when you know the subject personally. I did not know my father. My brother and I were eight and six respectively the early spring morning he died.

My memories of him are vague, unfinished. I cannot distinguish fuzzy happenings from anecdotes, and stories told. Perhaps this is the major reason his portrait never advanced beyond what I call a "First Pass"—the initial stage, before deeper shades and brighter highlights are applied to achieve a sense of "aliveness." I suspect other factors are at play preventing completion of his likeness. His life was incomplete, cut short, unfinished. I will never know how his death irrevocably altered the course of my life.

Some memories never fade. I still can see my mother in the archway of my grandmother's front entrance, head down, eyes red-rimmed welling with tears, her legs barely able to support her, her mind racing—searching for words to tell us our father had died.

I remember how abruptly everything changed—like watching a movie where characters and plot suddenly make no sense. Your everyday story unravels. Nothing knits together. There is no going back. The plug is pulled, and color drains from your life.

I cannot recall his voice, his laugh, the way he walked, or the touch of his hand but his sudden absence was painfully palpable. I did not comprehend death's finality, nor did I understand how in a split-second, death would forever reshape my future. The handsome, mustached man, who peeked through the kitchen window mugging funny faces before entering the house from a day's work, was simply no more.

I remember school crayons and construction paper and Father's Day cards that never went home. I remember the quiet that settled over our little home—the long silences, the emptiness, the loss of laughter. But, I also remember hope! Childhood hope. Childhood dreams that assured me he was playing baseball with kids in heaven as he had played with me.

I see him every morning. His unfinished likeness stares at me in the bathroom mirror. No memories surface. It's a bridge too far. Nevertheless, in some strange, indefinable way, his portrait silently stirs within me a timeless bond between father and son—an *undying love* spanning decades of death's separation. Childhood has come and gone. I no longer dream about him. Yet every so often something niggles at the edges of who I am. There will always be something unfinished about me.

Borrowed Memories

He has no face, no touch, no voice; they hide inside
bleak memories—the smoke and mirrors of stories told
set free of facts by fantasies that bleed between the lines.
He stares from faded photographs in grainy shades
of black and white. A snapshot of a homburg hat, of wide lapels,
deep dark eyes, a black mustache o'er silent lips that
cannot speak my name. Yet wispy thoughts of baseball mitts and
boxing gloves, of circuses, of silliness and childhood games
rise up from dusty boyhood dreams and say,
"I am not gone."
A thousand years have come and gone, and I have lived beyond his time,
eclipsed the pain of death's dark night when he no more returned
and dried a million mother's tears that love had drained away.
So long ago, so far away, so sure this pain was drowned,
I'm suddenly a child again, a lonely little boy again
whose father can't be found.
"Daddy!" "Oh Daddy!" A million miles away
tears unshed for countless years
now flow and cry your name.

Spliced

Saturday serial.[16] *Matinee. Fifteen cents. Grainy. Black and white.*
Scratchy lines. Scratchy dialogue. Roy socks the bad guy.
Down he goes. Two more rush him. Punch! Pow! Wham Bam! Wow!
KO-ed! His white hat undisturbed. What a GUY!
Shots ring out. Roy pulls Dale to safety. Clouds of dust.
Thundering hooves. The Garret boys ride straight for him guns
    blazing. Six-shooters jump into Roy's hands firing eighteen
    shots but who is counting? Besides, I'm there with him.
I'm in the film. NO, I am the film. I am Roy and Roy is me
    and we win the day, gun barrels smokin'!
The Garret gang bites the dust. Dale runs to Roy's side.
Please DON'T sing! If you do, I'll not stay and
    see the film again. Gads! They're holding hands.
Don't KISS her, Roy! Gag! They're singing
    and suddenly all is lost, all is changed and so am I.

The projector's click and clack continues.
No, Dale. No, Roy. No, me. No, we. Just darkness.
Dark beyond dark. Ink. Starless. A cavernous panoply.
Stripped clean, winter trees stretch and strain
    their bony, fragile, fingers clawing the night for warmth,
    for bud, for bloom, for light amid gloomy stagnant air,
    dank, still, heavy, unforgiving. Wordless cries unheard,
    unanswered. Silence. Windless. Speechless.
Stealthy flying shapes—shadowy silhouettes that have no
    names sweep warmth away. The silence of their soundless
    wings chill my tiny bones and I am far from home,
    far, far away from anywhere I have ever been—a place I
    know not where, a place I have not chosen.
Numb. Alone. Confused. Where ARE you, Jesus?
Plot, characters, swept suddenly aside. The slicing of my life
    from what is known to all that is unknown.
A cold, crescent moon smirks its scary smile streaked by wispy,
    wormy clouds stealing warmth and light, and in my boyish mind,
    I know my life will never be the same.
I am six. My brother eight. A screech of tires.
A sickening squeal of twisted steel.
A life snuffed out before its time.
Daddy is dead. My life is spliced. I'm not in the film.
The film is me, and I cannot find my tears.

A Princess Who Hugs
Ashley McMurray

Miss (excuse me) "Princess" Ashley McMurray seldom fails to run up and hug me on Sundays at church. It is conditional of course; she must see me first. When she was younger, she would look past belt buckles and hips surrounding her to find me. It is a "royal ritual" that absolutely makes my day! Our hug usually is followed by a short litany: *"Guess what?"* she queries. *"I don't know, tell me."* And she does with great enthusiasm. A pithy news report of what has happened, will happen, or she hopes will happen. She is a loving extension of me. I am a loving extension of her and that's how it should be with everyone and everything!

I'm sure Ashley has her not-so-happy moments, but her friendly hugs instill joy in this senior citizen. Life's joy, at any age, is really a matter of 'letting go' and 'holding on." Letting go of 'self-inflation." Letting go of "the too muchness" and "too littleness" of self and holding on tightly to what really matters: the lively notes of love, caring, kindness, compassion, and community played minute by minute, if we just stop to listen.[17]

Royal Embrace

She's pretty and frilly, a fashion-rite missy whose dresses
and tresses won't tolerate messes.
Ashley's the envy of all the princesses, whose graces and faces
in faraway places can never compete
with her smiles and embraces.
Her sweetness and neatness and downright completeness
will leave you just speechless when she comes your way.
For what can you say, it's not every day
a princess arrives and gives love away.

Reflection: Love Has Strings

In Matthew 19:27 (NRSV), Peter challenges Jesus, *"Look, we have left everything and followed you. What then will we have?"* Ironically, Peter's query is a contradiction in terms—his second sentence negates his first. The one thing Peter has not left behind is his hope for a payday! Peter wants to know if discipleship is worth the cost. Too often, service and love beg a "this for that" invoice.

Love has strings, each labeled, "BECAUSE." We love this or that, him or her (whatever) "because" their intrinsic worth warrants love. The doctrine of *Christian Assurance* affirms God's love is unconditional, uncaused, unmerited, unmitigated. Accordingly, Divine grace is completely free of strings or causative factors. "Because" flies out the window.

Perhaps, not. Unconditional love is a beautiful concept. It has rolled off my tongue in sermons preached and classes taught, but like Peter's query it is a contradiction in terms. Why? Because love *is* a condition. From this perspective, unconditional love is not love at all. God loves us "because" *we belong to God!* Metaphorically, God is the womb of existence. Parenthood (divine and otherwise) is an irrevocable condition of *belongingness*—a loving relationship capable of overwriting the vilest decisions and actions of one's children. There are exceptions of course, but parental love and forgiveness more often than not triumphs over a child's wayward lifestyle. Existential belongingness is the core of parenthood biological and otherwise. Bottom line?

> *"For I am convinced that neither death, nor life, nor angels, nor rulers,*
> *Nor things present, nor things to come, nor powers, nor height, nor*
> *depth, nor anything else in all creation, will be able to separate us from*
> *the love of God in Christ Jesus our Lord."* Romans 8:38-39 NRSV

My children can do nothing to sever my love for them and our mutual belongingness. I love them *because* they are mine, and they love me *because* I am theirs. They are a living part of me. We are living parts of each other. Love always has strings.

Make Us Vulnerable

How is it done, God? How do you love the unlovable?
Why do you persistently reach out to us, when our response
*   is habitually lethargic or vacant?*
What patience! What wonder! Help us to receive your grace.
Deep within our selfness we know why we fail to do so.
*   It's a matter of head over heart—our unwillingness*
*   to be debt free. Sweep away our self-sufficiency.*
Make us vulnerable, once again. Rebirth in us the innocence of
*   childhood that celebrates wonder and joy free of cost.*
For then, and only then, will we discover anew
*   the blessings of your grace.*

One Note

Alive beneath my feet, above gray clouds and deepest space, creation's
cosmic symphony plays discordant melodies. Life, death, gain, loss, unity,
disunity, chaos wed to harmony—the chorus rages on. Vibrating strings
of energy. Pulsing whirling galaxies stretching to infinity beyond my sight
and sound. Cascading rhythms. Cadence undefined reverberates natal
suns, the silent death of distant stars—their fading light now reaching us
eons lost and gone. Swirling spiral nebula. Planets, rocks, people spun
from boundless stardust. And deep within my fingertip—a cosmos housed
within. Modes and modulations. Countless cells and molecules, swirling,
spinning, crackling with life. Evolution's melody, stripped of tears and
laughter, plays on and I am but one note.

Word Magic

"Let there be light and there was light" casting all in bold relief.
Word magic—shaping past, present, and future. Words piercing heart,
mind, soul. Words that live again, breathe again, soar, dance, and sing
again on wings of choice and chance. Accolades. Critiques. Acceptance.
Rejection. Wounds received and given. Safe. Unsafe. Stripped clean of
self-obscuring. You, me, grass, trees, creatures great and small, formed
by vowels and consonants—the utterance of God's love. Come, speak
NEW words of healing hope. Forgiving words. Redemptive words. Words
that wash the gray away, that cleanse the soul and point the way to
kinder days where you and I are one. Words—self-realizing,
transforming, restoring! Say them, live them, set them free, grant them
space to shape and serve. Love's words—empowered to do their bidding,
deeper than deep, lighter than air, their whispers ever ringing.

Unpredictable
Ayla McMurray

Ayla McMurray's portrait warrants several possible titles: *"Catch Me If You Can," "Energy Unlimited," "My Dance, NOT Yours," "Cuteness Wins,"* to suggest but a few. If there is a singular argument against predestination, you are looking at it. Miss Ayla McMurray is very much her own person. Ten minutes with this fascinating young lady and you will know the world she will occupy will not be boring or "ordinary." Curious, intelligent, and inquisitive, Ayla's enthusiasm meter is high, and my guess is it will not wane in years to come. A mixture of assurance and shyness, Ayla likes her own space. Her imagination, determination, creativity, humor, and spirit of adventure will contribute meaningfully to life whatever path she chooses. I am predicting great things for this young miss.

Like sister, Ashley, Ayla also gives hugs, but on *her terms*. Her hug sharing moods are serendipitous, sometimes a *robotic response* to her sister's generosity. Her mother, Lyda, oversees Ayla's Sunday fashion debuts. Once home, I envision smudged T-shirts, stained shorts, sneakers, sandals or bare feet as her wardrobe. Ayla doesn't sleep. She collapses. She can charm herself out of just about any situation. I know she can with me.

Whirlwind

So unpredictable, intrepid, invisible, her speed's so incredible she seems everywhere. The wind in her hair blows bows through the air but she doesn't care if they're here or there. She dances and prances and takes silly chances. She giggles and wiggles and gives funny glances. Who winds her up? Does her spring ever break? When does she sleep? Does her mom get a break? Don't call out her name if she's playing a game, she'll plug both her ears and go on just the same. Her dad can console her, but no one controls her. She flops into bed when her feet become lead, and chatters on matters that come to her head till her eyes finally close when her battery is dead. The world is just waiting for someone like her, who thinks for herself and knows that for sure the problems we're facing she'll work at erasing. Preacher? Teacher? Candlestick maker? Pilot? Professor? Colonel or major? Whatever she does, regardless her path, just be aware, she'll be "CHIEF OF STAFF."

Cacophony

If I could hear a drop of rain sliding down a windowpane,
    a spider's dance on silver strands spun in silence end for end.
If I could hear a blade of grass crushed beneath my quickened step,
    the kiss of wind upon my face,
    the sizzling sound of sinking sun so soon asleep
    and seaward bound, its final gasp of lingering light
    —the drowning of the day.
If I could hear the softening hush of midnight stars,
    the rising of a harvest moon, a morning's resurrection
    when night is rolled away.
But I have lived a million years with ears that mute creation's sounds
    where miracles and songs abound that sing such mysteries
    —the whisper of conception when chromosomes in sympathy
    blend in perfect harmony the music of new life.
What happened to my infant ears
    that heard the beat of angels' wings
    and daily paused to wonder?

Life Everlasting?

Life everlasting? What of this shallow hope for endless days
    where sunsets cast no glorious rays,
      no sweet good-byes, no inky nights, no daily trials arising,
      for all is bliss, all wounds are healed, no pain, no death, no crying.
Who would abide this timeless yawn—this sleepy "now"
    stretched far beyond our searching?
Endless days seek no home, no hills to climb, no race to win,
    no deadlines drawn, no "would" or "could" or "should have been"
    —a measureless now where victory has no meaning?
Take heart. A bright new day awaits. A day of resurrection.
    A day when all shall rise again like he who rolled death's stones away.
    Not of blood and bone or heavenly home,
      nor pearly gates and golden streets, but one of health and healing.
    A day where every breath we take is savored as a blessing.
    A day of life beyond our dreams of countless days,
      where every hour holds hope and praise
      not *there and then* but *here and now*, at last, for our partaking.
Each day we die a thousand deaths
    and rise anew awakening, with eyes that see,
    hearts that feel, and ears that hear hope's melody
    and sing of love's reviving.

The Winds of Change Stir Every Age

The winds of change stir every age and cannot be restrained
    nor can the maps we've drawn of God divinity contain.
Our wanting words, our treasured texts, our tenets firmly claimed
    cannot hold fast within their grasp a God of many names.

Salvation comes alive in us when we unlock faith's door
    and step beyond our strained beliefs, horizons to explore.
Here gender roles and differences no longer segregate.
Every soul has equal worth and freedom to participate.
Christ's peace is not constrained by cultural points of view
    nor does it dwell in lofty scripts or creeds once claimed as true.
Peace comes alive in you and me in what we say and do
    to live the meaning of God's grace restoring life anew.

Not So High

Our girls watched "The Friendly Giant," which the online encyclopedia Wikipedia describes as "A Canadian children's program that aired on CBC from 1958 to 1985. It featured three main characters: a giant named Friendly who lived in a huge castle, along with his puppet animal friends Rusty (a rooster who played a harp and lived in a book bag hung by the castle window) and Jerome (a giraffe)." Each show began with Friendly inviting children to "Look up! Look way up."[18]

"Look up! Look WAY up!"
TV's Friendly Giant would say.
A good opening for a children's program.
A good opening for theological exploration.
Are you a friendly giant, God?
Are you in, out, above, beyond, or WAY up?
Have we labeled you omniscient, omnipotent, divine
*   —shaped you in our image—unmeasured, unconfined*
*   —a friendly giant spinning dreams death shall end its time?*
Magic begs no promise. Acceptance is it song.
Look up! Look WAY up! Omnipotence is "Friendly."
"Rusty" plays his harp. "Gerome" hums along.
Look down. WAY down. Their song sung. The credits roll.
"Friendly" will be back tomorrow.
Same time. Same station. Same song.

When lights go out and life tumbles in,[19]
*   when prayers are monologues and tragedy wins,*
*   when few get more and more get less—and we humbly quip,*
*   "God knows best"—the Giant isn't friendly!*
God, how can you be? We've granted you infinity.
Exchanged magic for your mystery.
Look up. Look down. Look all around. Look in the mirror.
Stretch a little, look WAY up—not so high you mute"Friendly's"cry,
*   "My kingdom lives within you. It's here. It's now.*
*   Not there and then, not feathered wings nor pearly gates.*
*   It dwells not in your mystic dreams. It's birthed by hope.*
*   It rises within. Its invoice is tears. Its hurts, mended. Its doors, open.*
*   Its balm, forgiveness. Its joy is peace, acceptance, community.*
*   Its magic is kindness and love. Look up! Look down!*
*   Look everywhere!"*

Inquiring Mind–Warm Heart
Bob Mesle

Men fear thought as they fear nothing else on Earth—more than ruin, more even than death. Thought is subversive and revolutionary, destructive and terrible; thought is merciless to privilege, established institutions, and comfortable habits; thought is anarchic and lawless, indifferent to authority, careless of the well-tried wisdom of the ages. Thought looks into the pit of hell and is not afraid. Thought is great and swift and free, the light of the world, and the chief glory of humanity.
—Why Men Fight (Bertrand Russell)[20] adapted.

My friendship with C. Robert (Bob) Mesle, retired professor of philosophy and religion at Graceland University, Lamoni, Iowa, is a long-distance relationship cultivated by Facebook and Bob's book, *Process Theology: A Basic Introduction*. Bob, an avid volleyball player, is indeed a thinker, teacher, player, and I should add, a "baker!" Though we have not shared more than five minutes of face-to-face conversation, I deeply respect this man who has dedicated his life to influencing and transforming students and caring for friends and strangers alike. I regret not having the privilege of being one of his students. Rather than describe him in my words, here are his words:

"My father taught me that the way to do theology is to ask, "Is that what a truly loving God would be like? Is that what a truly loving God would be doing in the world?" These questions are equally relevant whether you 'believe in God' or not because they are vital questions about our own commitment to love and justice. What would WE be like if WE were truly loving? If WE were truly loving and just, what would WE be doing in the world? (Dad also taught us that when camping, always leave the campsite cleaner than it was when you arrived and leave enough wood for the next group's first fire. They might arrive cold and wet.)

My father also taught me that we must love intelligently. Many Buddhist stories drive this point home. The Bodhisattva, Avalokitesvara, is often depicted as having many arms, and each hand has an eye in it. We need many arms and hands to help relieve suffering in the world. But the hand needs to see, to understand, or else good intentions can cause much harm. Influenced by Eastern thought, I tend to reframe my father's words (love intelligently) as "Seek compassionate wisdom," which I take as a mission statement for my own life and in my teaching. I continue to cherish the values I learned in my Christian family, church, and tradition, but I believe we can no longer imagine that one faith or wisdom tradition has an exclusive claim to truth, wisdom, justice, or love. We must find ways to continue to value our own roots, but in ways which give us the wings to fly out into the larger world of wisdom traditions and their visions of loving justice."

A Breath of Truth

Truth! We probe and pursue it. We strive to possess it when all the while it seeks to possess us. Disturbing, perturbing, we rejoice in it, weep in it, turn toward it, often at the cost of self-inflated perceptions. What did Jesus say? "The truth shall set you free." Free to die and live again! More than sacred texts, lofty thoughts, or creedal declarations, truth is death and resurrection. The death of little gods we dance to. The death of comforting concepts, tired definitions, and immaculate perceptions. Truth is the resurrection of new hopes, new joys, new possibilities. Truth rolls stones away! Fresh air comes in and life begins again.

Reflection: Abiding Trust

Faith and belief are not synonyms. Beliefs are declarations—*propositional statements* articulating deeply held convictions. We sing them, say them, preach and pray them, and thank God, we change them. Faith, on the other hand, is not adherence to a list of beliefs. Faith is *in-vocational*. Faith invokes or calls us to continually re-formulate beliefs when challenged by new understandings. Faith calls us to be hope-filled amid life's heartaches and unevenness. Faith is abiding trust in the present and future, free of fear.

If, God Were Not

What if, God were not and every thought and dream you sought
*   were wispy curls of hope?*
What if prayers slipped silently away and found no home,
*   no place to stay, no way to bless or burden?*
What if chaos ruled, and randomness sprinkled stardust into life?
And what if chance spun webs of thoughts
*   and consciousness birthed eternal yearnings?*
What if holy words on onion skin were blessed beyond their meaning
*   —the printed faith of earthly scribes passed down for our revering?*
What if angels had no wings, no songs of praise in starlit skies,
*   no babe for our adoring?*
What if Christ was but a name—a dream—a savior of our making?
The hymns we sing, the lessons taught, the sermons preached,
*   were all for naught? No heaven. No hell.*
*   No magic spells. No crown of jewels awaiting.*
Would we give a helping hand, a crust of bread, a word of hope and healing?
Would we place ourselves at risk to stop the world from bleeding?
Would strangers be our friends, and strive for love's safekeeping?
Would GOOD'S whisper stir in us or would its voice be fleeting?
Would we be good for "goodness' sake" and sacrifice our give and take
*   and find that God remains aflame*
*   for "GOOD" is but God's longer name?*

When Truth Knocks

"What is truth?" Pilate asked, and so do I.
At times, truth clearly shouts its name.
No wondering, no guessing. Simple. Plain.
"Unvarnished," as the saying goes.
Truth's neon sign blinks night and day
*   and burns the grays of doubt away,*
*   and does not shine unnoticed.*
Who could miss its siren song, deviate from what is known,
*   discerned, and better yet, agreed with?*
Truth's a friend when it sings my song,
*   but what of truth that is not mine,*
*   whose haunting melody and rhyme never finds me home?*
Patiently, persistently, truth knocks at my door
*   echoing its litany, "Search for something more."*

God Beyond God

They keep dying! These gods I thought I knew.
Gods I talked to. Gods I strained to hear.
Gods forever watching, waiting, anticipating,
*   protecting me in miraculous ways unseen.*
Convenient gods—dancing to my tune,
*   showing up, silently pointing the way.*
"Color-me-good-Sunday school-gods"
*   —tucked safely in my small corner bidding me to shine.*
And shine, I did: a faithful child, a questioning teen,
*   a naïve adult with faithful gods always on call,*
*   ready at a moment's notice to bend the universe just for me.*
Until the magic slipped away. Curtain down. Show over.
No walking on water. No sight to the blind.
No halting the sun at the raise of a hand.
Long on promises, short on delivery,
*   these little omnipotent gods keep dying.*
And so, they must! Any god that can be killed, should be.
So, where to from here? To the God beyond god!
A God of surprises! A God in process, leaning forward.
A God, free of excuses, freed from omnipotence.
A God who weeps with those who weep,
*   sings with those who sing, prays with those who pray,*
*   and dreams life's hopeful dream that grace will have its way.*
A loving-living God, who never dies when we do.

Fragility

Logic draws its lines and boxes,
*   while reason shouts aloud its name till little else is heard.*
Wonder shrinks inside me— deity and mystery desperately unnamed.
What lies beyond the boundaries of mind and soul and heart?
Have I thrown too much away? Are there missing parts?
The hope of immortality? The prayers that slip away?
To whom? To what? And why? And where? The counting of my days?
Where has all the magic gone? Has it been for naught?
The dances and the liturgy, the crafting of the homilies,
*   the lessons learned and taught?*
Something shaped by more than hope.
Something more than ecstasies, than holy writ and fantasies.
Something here inside of me will not let me go.
A fragile faith that will not wane.

There or Not There?

Theism, deism, pantheism, or "NO-ISM?"
I'm reading a book that says you don't exist, God. Maybe you've read it.
I find myself nodding in agreement and shouting, "Right on!"
He's saying things I've said myself, and things I've never said.
He hopes "religious readers who pick up his book
*   will be atheists when they put it down."*
Time will tell. So far, and it's early yet, we're on the same page.
Compelling arguments—persuasively written:
*   A world without religion resolves a lot of wars. CHECK!*
*   Respect for religion trumps respect for humanity. CHECK!*
*   The Bible gives you bad press, God. CHECK!*
*   You're not a celestial magician. CHECK!*
*   Theological opinions are not facts. CHECK!*
We have such a love affair with facts!
There are plenty between these pages and more to follow.
I have much to learn—as does the author.
That's what makes the journey worth taking!
Believers and nonbelievers keep nailing jelly to certainty's wall.
Life is more than facts, at least, it is for me.
Certitude is overrated. "The heart has reasons
*   that reason does not understand" (thank you, Pascal).*
Do the math—an endless stream of probabilities
*   swimming in evolution's sea of time and space*
*   could sprinkle us into existence—a momentary wink*
*   or cosmic blip, soon or never to be repeated.*
What then is at stake? Belief has everything to gain and nothing to lose?
*   Disbelief has everything to lose and nothing to gain?*
*   A tired argument—easily dismissed.*
The question remains: to whom are my prayers addressed?
Are you there, here, somewhere, anywhere hearing this, God?
Is this a monologue? Most often when I pray, I am talking to myself.
So, if you're not there God, what do I stand to lose?
At the very least some interesting conversations.
A fascinating book! Maybe, you wrote it.

Keeping Roads Open
Barbara Mesle

For Barbara Hiles Mesle, retired professor of English at Graceland University, "why, how, and what if?" are life-long queries. Fueled by her love for literature and life, questions serve "to understand herself, others, and this world better." A lover of art, music, film, and literature, Barbara shares husband Bob's passion to "live life's questions" and drink in its wonder.

As with Bob, my friendship with Barbara has blossomed largely through Facebook. Nothing intimidates an amateur wordsmith more than a brilliant English professor, so I am counting on Barbara to focus more on my drawings and less on my prose. Barbara's own words share but a hint of why Bob and others adore this intelligent and wonderfully gifted lady:

"One purpose of Art, broadly defined, is to keep the Roads open between the 'Seen' and the 'Unseen,'" said Elizabeth Barrett Browning. I believe this idea. I am not an elitist about Art (read that film, literature, music, painting, etc.). Art is for everyone. I love poetry for the same reason I

love baseball—they force me to 'go slow!' A lot of life is due to both chance and choice. I have worked very hard to create and sustain a career and family in my life I enjoy so much. I do not agree that destiny makes house calls. But Gratitude is also something I try to cultivate daily. I am so blessed to have students and work I care about. I love reading and traveling. I worry about the health of our planet—partly because I have four beloved grandchildren. While I know that this world is full of Woe, I also believe deeply that it is full of Wonder, as long as we remember, as Barbara Kingsolver once wrote, to put on Hope every morning along with our shoes."

Unconfined[21]

Thank God, for poetry! Not its rhythm, meter, or rhyme,
nor even its strained beauty.
No, celebrate its ambiguity—its highs and lows stretching for the sublime,
its faltering phrases unequal to what it strives to convey
in language, divine: the pulse of the heart,
the dreams of the mind, the wordless cries of the soul.
Poetry, and prose—no matter-of-factness,
no recipes or formulas to make mystery mute.
Poetry, in all its artful forms, is faith's bright window.
Brushstrokes, canvas, wood, and stone.
Symphonies, cacophonies, notes on a page,
never quite blue enough, true enough,
wanting, taunting, always yearning for more.
A clear note sounded, a rough edge rounded.
A marriage of meanings when words newly wed
suddenly say what can never be said:
the telling of God that remains untold.
A dab here, a dab there—just a hint
a splash of serendipity sprinkled on canvas,
an unsurpassed aria, a wispy word or two
wrapped in metaphor where mind, heart, and spirit play.
Faith measured is faith restrained.
Set it free! Let it ring out in fanciful verse,
a singer's song, an artist's sketch, a blush of color, a liturgical dance.
Thank God for poetry—good, bad, wanting and waiting,
stretching and straining, never content, never indifferent;
its soiled song unwilling to be contained.

Playing the Echoes

Play the echoes, the "do-overs," your fourth and fifth swing at bat.
Better yet, bat again—make the best of the worst of times.
It's not a matter of wiping life's slate clean.
Let the stains remain—the who, when, where and why of choices
*   made, sweet or sour—the essence of your living.*
Chalk dust sins fade in time. Let them serve, not sever.
Release their tired claims. Flush guilt away!
No replays, reruns, painful repetitions.
Stop playing yesterday's game.
Just, "Play the echoes." Try again. Rise again.
"Put on hope." No more final innings.

Tread Softly

Tread softly friends, the ground is one with us
*   and aches from the weight of staggered steps*
*   o'er beaten paths dug deep by dead understandings.*
A journey that sees no new horizons,
*   a bumbling, slumbering sleep-walk of everydayness,*
*   every twig, pebble, and leaf known and named,*
*   trampled down by familiarity.*
A tomorrow of endless yesterdays, a sky ablaze with smiling sun,
*   no darkened hues nor nights of new revealing,*
*   for all is said and done in loops rerun by measured rules*
*   that soothe a soul numb to new beginnings.*

Tread softly friends, for dreams are trampled underfoot
*   far beneath hope's ceiling.*
Dance lightly, raise them up, let them breathe
*   freed from memory's sleeping. The "never realized" still has voice,*
*   and spells anew your yearnings. Tread joyfully friends.*
New steps await your path with promises of pain and joy,
*   holding on and letting go—life's sanctities and mysteries,*
*   ecstasies and agonies, of questions never ending,*
*   that resurrect your sleeping hope*
*   and stirs your soul's awakening.*

Outside the Lines

Pin it down. Prove it. Paint within the lines.
Domesticate the mystery with facts and quotes sublime
*   of ancient creedal recipes that boggle thinking minds.*
We cannot squeeze divinity within such sacred tomes.
Theology is poetry, not certitude that rhymes
*   salvation's sweet security in some ethereal home.*
Peer behind faith's narrative; read between the lines
*   —the glory of each story, its facts cannot define.*
Fish to feed five thousand. Sight for searching eyes.
Empty tombs and parables, poetic prayers and miracles,
*   rest not in literal lines of texts defining life divine.*
Escape their denotation, release their connotation
*   —loss and grief, joy and gain, peace and pain.*
LOVE lives and lights each sacred life.
All is incarnation! Every breeze divine.
Free tradition's formulas that seek to quell the night
*   with lists of strict requirements defining wrong and right.*
Embrace each grace-filled moment. Let kindness rule the day.
The God in me, the God in you—this Spirit that resides in us
*   is called by many names and paints outside the lines.*

Something Beyond

It's all well and good.
Toss the Ol' Man away—the Guy in the Sky,
*   the "sweet bye and bye,"*
*   the baker, the shaker, the candle-stick maker.*
But what of sweet mysteries of starlight and song,
*   of soft summer breezes, of skylarks and dawn*
*   painting the morning with colors undone?*
What do we worship and whom do we praise
*   if the extent of our faith are hands that we raise?*
Is there room for "awe" and wonder in our daily dance?
Is the music but ours, just a matter of chance,
*   a blending of atoms, over eons and more*
*   or does something beyond sprinkle notes on the score?*

Beach Boys

Hand in Hand
Owen and Ian Campbell

If I had patent rights to sand pails and shovels, Warren Buffet's wealth would be a drop in the bucket (pun intended). What children have not erected sandcastles, dug moats, carved mighty rivers, watched waves roll in and wash their work away only to start digging and building again? If art forms have any historical staying power, then sand art shaped by tiny minds overflowing with imagination, and confidence is one of them.

Creativity fills canvases, taps keyboards, sings arias, conquers space, sews on buttons. Everything from whittling a stick to designing a skyscraper calls for innovation and artistry. Music's home is not a Stradivarius; its residence is the musician. A thousand recipes of chili inspire a thousand more. Creativity never sleeps or plays favorites. It resides in every blade of grass, boundless swirling nebula, each string of energy animating all that is,

48

which means it resides in you—discovered and undiscovered.

"Creative? Not me!" you say. *"Yes, you!"* Don't throw away your bucket and shovel. You are far more creative than you think you are. Even Jesus scribbled in the sand. Mind you, an angry throng intent on stoning an adulteress interrupted his playtime.

Reading between the lines I think he dropped his pail and shovel, gazed quickly at the woman and whispered, *"Get out of here! NOW!"* I hear shouts shrinking to murmurs—the mob suddenly silent, stunned by Christ's calmly stated indictment, *"Adultery? Am I missing something? Shouldn't a man be included here? Tell you what, let the purest among you cast the first stone!"* I think Jesus picked up his pail and shovel and said to the woman, *"Learn from your mistakes, I know I have. Get on with your life. Go! There's far more to you than you could possibly imagine!"*

Look closely at my rendering of Owen and Ian Campbell. I love the obvious fun, freedom, and shared single-mindedness they apply to their sand creation. It's playtime. And more than playtime! It's together time. I love the memories it evokes. I can almost feel my plastic shovel and the sheer joy of knowing *whatever* I created would be wonderful, despite wind and wave. I wonder, does God smile while digging black holes, scribbling spiraling nebulae, strings of energy and billions of galaxies dancing in the ink of space? I can hear God chuckling with glee, shaping and reshaping this cosmic sandlot of which we are but a very, tiny part. Think of it. Every grain of sand on every planet in every universe, moment for moment, wave upon wave, is perpetually evolving. Who or what else could play with countless pails and shovels for eternity? And isn't it marvelous that we *can learn* from our mistakes (I'm sure God does) and get on with our lives, because there is so much more to us than we ever imagined!

Ȟand in Ȟand

Don't ask, "Who's in charge?" These two work together
   shaping and making a dream they're creating
   with shovel and pail and sifting white sand.
They're building a castle without any hassle.
It's laughter they're after; not what they've planned.
And should their construction meet with destruction
   there's no interruption when waves hit the sand.
The name of the game is build it again.
The mansion's erection is not the attraction;
   it's playing together through thick and through thin,
   each helping the other to make sure they win.
So, it's not just two shovels, two pails, and some sand;
   it's giving and taking and never forsaking
   that everything's better when you work hand in hand.

Scribbles in the Sand

Yahweh's crowd. Yahweh's hands and feet,
Yahweh's one-sided righteousness.
The jeers! The chants! The judgment!
Pausing, waiting, anticipating.
She stands accused alone.
A pious crowd hangs back bemused,
  but no one casts a stone.
Someone doodles in the dust, and eagerness is lost.
Were they reading what he wrote?
A word? A phrase, a caustic note?
"Let the purest begin. Clean of blame and sin.
Cast your righteous stones, closer to home."

Scribbled lines scattered in the sand.
Thank God there's not a single sentence written by his hand.
No, sermon notes, no hillside quotes, no formulas
  for miracles or copyrighted parables.
We've wrapped him in divinity and snuffed out his humanity.
If we could find one word he penned
  we'd worship it, instead of him.
On second thought, a phrase or two might set him free
  from wanting words have shaped him be.

Shadow Land

Shadow land—neither dark nor dour, neither bleak nor disheartening.
Just this mix of knowing and not knowing,
  my seeking and searching, where questions plead and prance,
  where joy and hope and sorrow dance—each following, then leading.
A neutral place, a sacred space, where sunlight's shafts burn haze
  away, where clouds are white and sometimes gray,
  where night and day are one. "Walk in the Light" the chorus sings,
  a text that is disturbing, for God walks also in the dark, abandons
  not my inky nights, my shadow land of living. Here, prayers are stripped
  of saccharine praise and endless self-petitions.
Here, creedal inconsistencies no longer bind the soul.
Here, tragedies and victories, miracles and mysteries birth narratives of
  newfound hope, I struggle to divine. Amid life's ambiguities,
  I dance with One who owns the dark, and bids my soul to shine.

Deadly Serious

Penelope says my writing needs to lighten up, God.
*   Too dark. Too brooding. Too much angst*
"Write some happy prayers. Whatever happened to joy?"
We can do that, can't we. Let's talk about dying.
No, I'm not rebelling. I'm not pouting and mumbling,
"I'll show you!" I'm deadly serious.
Look, there are Christians who want to live forever,
*   who don't know what to do with themselves*
*   on a rainy afternoon.*
There are things inside us that need dying
*   to make more room for joy.*
As poet Wallace Stevens says, "Death is the mother of beauty."
Mortality shouts, "Make the most of every minute;
*   squeeze all you can from life, taste every drop."*
We ignore life's waning clock and fail to hear its ticking.
We think our days are endless, until, of course, they're not!

So here is today's lesson:
Slept in this morning! Unusual? Unheard of!
*   **There's joy in that!***
Didn't shave. Big deal. So, what!
*   **There's joy in that!***
Drank milk from my cereal bowl. First time in years!
Got a mustache! Childish! Impetuous!
*   **There's joy in that!***
It has stopped raining. The sun is pushing through.
We're going for a walk. We'll smile, hold hands,
*   look at each other, and whisper words unspoken.*
*   **There's joy in that!***
Come with us, God, if you have the time.
Better yet, take the time! You're far too busy.
Lighten up! Laugh a little! No angst. No brooding. Cheer up!
I'm going to live all day today; I can hardly wait.
*   There's JOY in that! I'm just dying to!*

Soul Mate
Penelope Prior Belrose

How do you say the unsayable? Words are too anemic to convey our highest thoughts and deepest emotions. There is always slippage, which is to say, this tribute to my wife, Penelope, will be overdone yet underdone.

Penelope Lynne (Prior) Belrose has loved, blessed and encouraged me for more than half a century. She is not "the wind beneath my wings"; she is (awkward grammar) my wings, my up when I'm down, my strength when I'm weak, my guide when I'm lost, my anchor when adrift. When she reads this, she will roll her eyes and say, "Eliminate all this fluffy stuff. Just say, you love me." OK, I love you! I love you because your physical beauty is surpassed only by an inward grace that blesses friend and stranger with compassion and kindness.

Love begs a response. In other words, my love for Penelope also is conditioned by her love for me. Penelope knows the more and the less of me and I know the more and the less of her. Our union is not perfect. Perfection has no hills to climb, no epiphanies, no grand hopes.

The heart of our relationship is intimacy—an open, mutual, sharing of each other's strengths, weaknesses, and foibles free of condemnation. Intimacy involves celebrating those unique, quirky peccadilloes—inside jokes and phrases, certain looks, a readiness to laugh at ourselves and each other that are lost in translation to others. Our love is rooted in reciprocal trust, honesty, and patience that strives to bring out the best in each other. In sum, our marriage is sustained by shared strengths, ethical values, and an abundance of good humor. We laugh a lot! And we cry a lot. We weather life's storms hand-in-hand seeking to understand the other's pain, honoring individuality and personal space, while helping the other to mend brokenness.

Brokenness is not at odds with wholeness. I am whole, but I am not complete. I am a work in progress. Wholeness is who I am (good and not so good) at any stage of me becoming me. Our love is more than chemistry; it is a willing choice to accept the other's incompleteness, which like one's own, is seeking constant repair. In this sense, brokenness is mended by beauty's echo bouncing back and forth over years of loving commitment that sees a young face in an old face, that accepts imperfection not as an easy truce but an opportunity for transformation through love that divides sorrows and multiplies joys.

The cosmos dances its mysterious choreography of randomness, order, life, death, and rebirth—a disjunctive *pas de deux* of harmony and disharmony in rhythm with each evolving note played by diversity. This dance, and our response to it, shapes who we are and who we may become. Fragmented relationships are mended by confession, forgiveness, reconciliation, and transformation. It is OK to not be OK, whenever OK means perfect and pristine. Penelope and I are incomplete, but we are whole. We dance to the uneven cadence of life's ambiguities and sudden startling joys. We occasionally step on each other's toes but are always in step with the other's highs and lows.

Love Beyond Acceptance

Love does not accept everything; it cannot, will not, must not!
Love cares for the condition of the beloved.
Love lays itself down, befriends, defends, amends the beloved.
Love's light disperses shadows. Acceptance ignores them.
Acceptance harbors no hurts, celebrates no joys,
    leaves "well enough" alone, calls for no transformation.
Its look-the-other-way litany pierces no hands or feet,
    weeps no tears of hope, rolls no stones away,
    begs no Easter mornings. True love tells it like it is.
It seeks higher ground. It defies all that's harmful at risk of rejection.
Its Shalom strives for the other's highest good whatever the cost
    —recompensed daily in an unquestioned willingness
    to sacrifice self for the other.

Imperfection

*Each life is a living letter filled with foibles, flaws, and failings, with hurts
and helps and hopes. A narrative of beauty, bliss, and brokenness with years
of tears and laughter spilling on each page. It's not a perfect plot, thank God.
Perfection has no legs; its landscapes never change. It quells life's drive to
seek for more and mutes hope's contemplation. Wholeness is here and now; it
seeks no flawless dream stripped of expectations. It measures who we are
each day free of condemnation. It bears the fractured soul; it points to paths
we've yet to tread of growth and transformation. It never seeks perfection's
face. It thrives where love and life abound in God's abiding grace.,*

Soft Sacrament

Each morning Penelope and I read to each other from separate books followed by a prayer for
the day. I used to "pray for a living" (smile) so she does the praying. Her prayer is not a
laundry list of petitions soliciting divine intervention but one of gratitude. It's the soft
sacrament that begins our day together.

She doesn't know it, but she prays with her hand.
Cupped in mine, I feel its warmth, its gentle touch,
*   the subtle rhythm of her finger pulsating in sync*
*   with this word and that as she prays our morning prayer.*
Neither long nor short. A word of thanks, a hope expressed,
*   thoughts of friends and strangers, a plea for peace,*
*   for war to cease, the cementing of our love. No shopping lists.*
No magic here. Just two souls entwined in sacred time
*   over breadcrumbs and cereal bowls.*
A prayer seeking, yet not seeking, saying, yet not saying.
A prayer answering its own desires, an utterance of faith fueling its
*   own fruition—a desire to serve the day.*
Here, ritual is wrapped in wonder, where words expressed
*   seek more than the heart's glow and the leaving of lists*
*   at Heaven's door. A brief, warm, touch—a soft sacrament*
*   where each sunrise two lovers become one again,*
*   where the sweet cadence of hope*
*   seeks the rhythm of our hands and feet.*

Reflection: Getting Through

Prayer is not a matter of getting through to God, but a heightened awareness that life's wonder and sacredness consistently is trying to get through to me. Such prayers arise serendipitously as a passing thought, a line of music, the sweep of a paintbrush, the writing of a poem, an idea lifted (up? out? within? without?), candlelight, uninhibited laughter, or awareness and support for the hopes and needs of others. This is not *anything-goes* relativism. These actions do not constitute prayer in and of themselves. They become prayer because they reconnect me with *the God in me, the God in others*, and the sheer wonder of life.

Prayer stretches hope into action. Prayer is silence and storm, solitude and togetherness. Spoken, unspoken, formally composed or extemporaneously expressed, prayer can be a lively awareness of life's wonder revealed through impromptu happenings that thrust open the windows of the soul: the flash of a robin's wing, a sip of sunlight, a stranger suddenly no longer a stranger, a sensual sweep of music, or that sudden catch in your throat in the presence of beauty. Prayer, in this sense, is a confession of universal communion and connectedness with all that is; the realization we are no less and no more than the stars above or blades of grass beneath our feet.

Each Life a Sanctuary

Far away, a temple stands, swirling spire, steel and stone, sparkling in the sun. More than silent sanctuary; its voice has many tongues. It longs for peace beyond its doors. It whispers day and night. It calls for caring hearts and hands to bring peace to life. Its ministries expand beyond the ground on which it stands, expressed in simple acts of grace wherever needs demand. No swirling spire, no shining steel, no shadow of the cross. WE are its hands and feet—living sanctuaries giving, receiving, learning, teaching, blessing and serving—walking, talking, listening, sharing, doing. Believer or non-believer, male, female, old, young, gay, straight, transgender, non-binary. Everyone and anyone who celebrates the worth of all souls and serves the better good, stands not in a cathedral's shadow but bears its healing light.

Love Does That

Anyone acquainted with Penelope would be surprised to discover she was once a shy, introverted, young lady so lacking in confidence that ordering a pizza was an anxiety-provoking event. No, I have not changed her. Thankfully, she is changing me. We are changing each other. There is more to the phrase "two shall become one" than we realize. *Love does that!* Love brings out the best in the beloved. Penelope is of her own making and our making. I do not remember how, when or where she threw angst out the window, but she did and does so every day. She has strengths, wisdom,

insights, and social skills I do not have. In social settings, I follow her like a puppy, leaning on her natural ability to make friends and initiate conversation and meaningful connections. Penelope is not hesitant to speak her mind. She tackles tasks and assignments I would never attempt and gets things done! She loves me, supports me, levels me off, raises me up and cares more for me than she does herself. *Love does that.* Penelope mentors others challenging them to do what they think they cannot do. She fearlessly assumes leadership roles. She serves meals to the homeless and organized a knitting group to provide hats for hospital preemies. She has served as a pastoral community outreach leader whose monthly goals over the years have contributed thousands of food and household items to our local Community Services League. Penelope is a member of "Dining for Women," a charitable program that contributes funds to aid women and children. Sounds perfect, doesn't she? She is to me. But then, *love does that!*

ђere ᴕhen Is Love

Two hands clasped, fingers knit, holding on, letting go,
touching, feeling, caressing, protecting.
Two lips meeting, two hearts beating rhythmically, uniquely
each to its own cadence.
Two lives united, yet separate—unchained by blind acceptance:
dreams of perfection, unfettered bliss,
and glassy seas unseasoned by life's storms.
Two lovers sealed by more than friendship, chemistry, sexuality,
but secured by sacred mutuality—the willingness to give all,
receive all, sunshine, shadow, fire and rain.
Each eager to say, "I'm sorry,"
pick each other up, dust each other off,
forgive, befriend, and defend.
Two souls who hold on and know when to let go,
for love releases as well as retains.

A God-shaped Hole[22]

There's a God-shaped hole in my heart filled with empty things—
   songs, sermons, hymns, and prayers, classes taught and taken,
   books read and underlined, tiny gods forsaken.
Important things, needful things that stretch the mind and soul,
   and yet these substitutes for Spirit's breath cannot fill the hole.
There's a God-shaped hole in my heart filled with empty things—
   good intentions never birthed, letters left unwritten,
   hopes and hunches still unsung, ears that failed to listen.
Important things, needful things that free and feed the soul.
But these achieved, less Spirit's breath, cannot fill the hole.
There's a God-shaped hole in my heart filled with empty things—
   important things, needful things—yet sweep them all away!
For God alone must fill this space; it's meant to be that way.
This silent, aching, sacred space softly sings my name,
   with Spirit's breath, it speaks to me and calls me o'er again,
   "Slow down my child, take rest my child,
   and pause to breathe my name; let emptiness refresh,
   renew, restore your soul again."
A God-shaped hole, a Love-shaped hole never fully filled
   —reminding me that piety and works cannot replace
   the emptiness that's always void without God's gift of grace.

Love Defeats the Calendar

Love never smothers but gently lifts the beloved into the floodlight of promise, potential, and grace. Standing close, yet not too close. Neither eclipsed by the other's shadow. Each freely bestowing breathing room, growing room—room for doubt, defeat, forgiveness, and renewal. Here then is Love most sacred: Love that's in it for the long haul. Love that hurts and heals. Love that defeats the calendar—that sees a young face in an old face. Love that divides sorrows and multiplies joy.[23] *Love tied tightly—knit forever securely by bonds of fidelity, forgiveness, freedom, and fruition.*

Meager Gifts

God, we have been awakened by your grace. Let us rub the sleep from our eyes that we may once more drink in the wonder of your creation of which we are but a part. Bless us beyond the meager gifts we offer. May we be constantly amazed by your love and may we amaze others with its wonder. Amen

A More Excellent Way

A more excellent way—not a perfect, unblemished way.
Not a "smile and get over it," Pollyannaish way,
   but a sustained sense of "at home-ness"
   with all that comes your way, the good and not so good
   woven within the wonder of the ordinary:
   a stranger's smile, a tear shed, a healing word,
   the awareness that shadows are sustained by sunlight
   and darkness is filled with the One who owns it.
A way where weakness is wed to strength,
   doubt and fear are playmates, and hope and faith are verbs.
A way where forgiveness begins with oneself drowning the past,
   cleansing the present and flowing freely into tomorrow.
A way filled with victories great and small, with dreams
   worth dreaming—a pouring out of who you were, are,
   and who you strive to be—a drenching of compassion
   and the joy of simple things. A "more excellent way" holds
   to all that's precious, releases that which binds,
   and stretches for what can be.
It's a way of living resolutely, honestly, and faithfully,
   amid the joy and junk of life where wounds are neither hidden,
   denied nor celebrated and perhaps never completely healed.

Edges

If I could just get the fold right. Even. No edges showing. The envelope waits.
Sized right. Now, just fold the letter at the right line of text hoping upon hope
the second fold will be even. Neat. Complete. No edges showing—everything
in its place. We try to do the same with you, God. Get the fold right. "Truth
Restored" the commercial claims. How tragic. Faith has become belief and
belief has become facts and facts have birthed certitude. Knowing has
replaced living. No ragged questions unanswered. God in a box or an
envelope. If I could just get the fold right—I would be God. What are you
smiling at? Are some edges showing?

ḣigḣ Finance–ḣigḣ Fidelity
Debashis Dey, "Jedi"

Have a five-minute conversation with nephew Debashis Dey and you will discover the "extraordinary in the ordinary." Debashis is a partner in White & Case LLP International Law Firm's Capital Markets Practice. If you watch one of his favorite films, "Margin Call," you may understand some intricacies inherent in Debashis's world of high finance. Then again, maybe not. The following is White & Case's Internet profile of Debashis:

"Widely recognized as one of the Middle East's leading capital markets lawyers, Debashis helps domestic and international clients to execute a spectrum of complex transactions. His works in the high strata world of international finance spanning more than 20 years of advising investment banks, corporates and governments on capital markets, securitization and structured finance matters, including Islamic finance sukuk transactions, regulatory capital transactions, commercial and residential mortgages and consumer finance. Debashis has led numerous product innovations in both conventional and Islamic finance. He is qualified in England and Wales, New York, British Columbia and Ontario, and executes deals in and across jurisdictions in the GCC (UAE, Qatar, Saudi Arabia), Europe, the US and Asia."[24]

Right! Got it? Not me. I can't count the change in my pocket. What Debashis does and how he does it, is beyond me. On the other hand, he might have difficulty explaining the Christological variance between "homoousia" or "homoiousia." (I do too, but just had to squeeze that in.)

Debashis is more than a globetrotting, international lawyer. He is a loving, dedicated husband, father, and a generous, loyal, down-to-earth friend. He loves what he does, but not at the cost of who he is. His successful career does not shape him; he shapes it. He resolves divergent issues, devises unique business plans, and creatively secures agreements that benefit all players—except, of course his competitors, who wish he was on their team.

The label "Jedi" after Debashis's name beat-out "Storm Trooper" and "The Force," by the narrowest of margins. Storm Trooper? The Force? Yes, he is a nice guy, but a *shrinking violet* would not last a day in his business. Of course, there is no "closing time" in the echelons of global finance. Success requires the tenacity of a Storm Trooper and willingness to rely upon The Force, circumspectly applied. It's a demanding business, that invariably requires tenacity in saying what needs saying.

Why the Star Wars speak? Because downtime can find Debashis side by side with son, Siddhartha, relying on The Force to defeat Darth Vader in a video game, constructing a Lego Millennium Falcon, cheering Siddhartha at karate and fencing class, or skiing with him and mother Julie, down the Alps. (They exercise consistently and are in great shape). Debashis also can be found in the kitchen preparing an epicurean delight (lamb is a specialty). Hobbies? Researching and collecting music, test-driving exotic sport cars (wife, Julie loves her secondhand Mini Cooper) collecting art, entertaining friends and expending any energy left over to live life to the fullest. Here is Debashis's initial response to my take on him:

> *"It is always daunting to read what someone else writes about you but given this is uncle Danny and given his genuine love for the people he surrounds himself with, I am willing to grin and bear it (even if I actually feel like hiding in the corner). If I were to make a personal observation, I would say the one consistent skill I try to apply is to learn at least one important lesson from those I keep close to me. Uncle Danny is one of those people, and in between long stories that he tells me (which, I ignore), he has some genuine gems that are worth gathering up and admiring at leisure. One of these is a lesson he once explained about memory, the passage of time, and the importance of friends in preserving who you are, who you were, and what you will be. I cannot do it justice here, but I can say that I honor that lesson (and polish that gem) with all my friends every time I can. I genuinely live my life by it—all from a little story he shared with me one night many years ago."*

JULIE ARTHURS DEY:

"Debashis is an avid reader of philosophy, history, graphic novels, syfy, etc. A lover of art, music, bistros, wine, and fine food, Debashis treats everyone with respect. He has never considered me as someone needing to be taken care of by a man.

Debashis is a person of great ambition and drive. His pursuit for excellence was instilled in him by his parents, who immigrated to three continents during his upbringing. For twenty-five years, I have seen his ambition evolve. He doesn't hesitate to help those in need and has been a great mentor to others.

Debashis has learned to realize that what he has accomplished in world finance law does not really apply at home. Siddhartha and I take our jobs seriously in reminding him of this, but we of course are proud of his vast achievements. Many view Debashis as a man of grandeur. What most people don't realize is that his pleasures really are simple. He spends what little free time he has doing such exciting things as: reading, movies, TV, working out, dining, skiing (well, that IS exciting). It's just that he prefers to do them with a martini in hand. Dry. With a twist. No olive. He is happy and wants those around him to be happy. Debashis doesn't waste life and surrounds himself with people he loves and appreciates. What also is not widely known about my husband is that he is truly a man of great conscience, more so than most people I know. He gives grandly and quietly and is considerate of others in his conduct of business and daily life. Many times, I have seen him go out of his way to help his friends or complete strangers. Sometimes his natural desire to help needs curbing—like when he gave directions to a stranger in Rome. Debashis does not speak Italian, nor does he have a great sense of direction; this is where my role comes in as his wife, 'the truth-teller.' Debashis is admired by many, but our cat, Meowie, has a serious feline crush on him. I am not kidding. It's embarrassing."

Stardust

LIFE—spun from scattered starlight woven together in the mutual fabric of creation. Ever evolving. Ever expanding. Contracting, pro-acting, God's cosmic dance. We are stardust! We ARE the earth! Walking, talking, breathing-earth. You, me, land, and sea—the same. Divided by idolatry—a myopic anthropology that places us far higher than we stand. We think our worth exceeds this earth—this home that gives us life.

Simply Share Them

Help us, God, to offer gifts of time, talent, and treasure, not counting cost.
Strike our names from attribution. Help us quietly rejoice as we "give thee
but thine own"—pressed down, shaken together, and overflowing,
You have authored all our gifts. May we not slice, dice, divide, or weigh
them, but simply share them. May we receive fully so we can fully give.

Syncopation

I wish I could talk to you. Say what needs to be said
    to lift the weight of wounding words that snuff out joy.
I wish I could hear your silent cries,
    strip your shield of saccharine smiles and sweet good-byes
    and syncopate the pulse of who you are with who I am
    —a mutual self who craves a kindred soul
        whose crumbling life falls and fails, yet rebuilds anew
        with bricks of understanding.
I wish I could see the "more" of you: your weathered dreams,
    your victories small, large and hoped for,
    the subtle fears that steal the night,
    your undiscovered gifts and graces yet to see the light.
Red, yellow, black, brown, shades of tan and white.
Prayer mats, crosses, swirling spires, saffron robes, holy fire,
    prophet, pilgrim, penitent, Wailing Wall and wailing souls,
    believer or non-believer.
You are me and I am You— more alike than different.

Reflection: The Way

   "I am the way, the truth and the life." But what of they who ritually bathe and pray five times a day? What of they who sound shofars, keep kosher laws and wedge their prayers in Wailing Walls? Some beat drums with spirit chants praising you with feathered dance. Some scribe circles in the sand with Mother-Earth in pentagrams. Others give you many names, many hands, and many feet while others walk an eight-fold path and seek to be "awake." Buddha's way, Yahweh's way, Allah's, Krishna's, Jesus's way! The way of death and resurrection. The death of isolation, revulsion, and self-deception that ours alone is the only way. The resurrection of the right arrangement of relationships with self, others, and creation. The way of joy, hope, love, peace, harmony amid diversity—faith's rainbow of sacred community where any way one sincerely worships praises life.

always in process ...

A Lady for All Seasons
Julie (Dey) Arthurs

Yes, niece Julie Arthur's portrait is UNFINISHED (the second one in this collection) because "this lady for all seasons," is perpetually in process. Julie doesn't just sip life, she savors it. Fun-loving by nature, Julie knows fun is an isolated event that ignites laughter and delight, while joy has staying power. Joy sustains us in good and not-so-good times. Joy, for Julie, is an attitude not simply an event.

Julie's smile is bright, wide, and contagious. Her bizarre sense of humor is spontaneous. Be prepared for (oh, wait, you can't be) slapstick, mugging, hilarious dancing, and boisterous off the wall one-liners that not only crack you up but reveal Julie's zest for life. Yet beneath her laughter flows a sustaining stream of hope amid life's ups and downs. Does she get angry? Does she lose it? Of course! Been there. Heard that. Seen that. Hallelujah! Too many people gunnysack their feelings. Not Julie. Hers is not a mindless, Pollyannaish, coat-hanger smile beaming, "Well I guess I can't do anything about that!" The words *can't,* and *complacency* are not in her dictionary.

Julie easily could play the role of Luke's "persistent widow" screaming for justice in the ear of the reluctant judge—not in terms of begging for attention but in getting it! Immediately! She is determined, strong-willed, and a force to be wary of where injustice begs speaking-up and taking, action!

Julie was administrative assistant at Deloitte (audit, consulting, financial, risk management, tax services), and a former administrative assistant at Transport Canada. She describes herself as "self-employed." Believe me, she is! If a role model for "the ordinary home-maker" exits, Julie doesn't fit it.

Husband Debashis, would agree he and Julie are each other's better half. Being a successful, international money market lawyer requires consistent globe-trotting. Julie is CEO on the home-front—managing dual residences (Dubai and London). It's a demanding task, which includes, among other responsibilities, hiring and firing household staff, balancing income and expenditures in both countries, maintaining, designing and overseeing major renovations, juggling calendar, travel, and appointment schedules, hosting frequent visitors, while she and Debashis parent their son, Siddhartha (whom she refers to as "the Boy," regardless of his age).

The first three letters of Julie's birth name, ARThurs, is a striking fit! Julie not only loves and collects art, she is a skilled and accomplished artist. She studied drawing, painting and animation at Emily Carr University of Art and Design, graphic design at George Brown College, and drawing at School of the Museum of Fine Arts, Boston. She says, "Seven years studying art was like winning the lottery of life." There is nothing in the world she wanted more. I love her work and wish she would squeeze more time from her schedule to pick up pencil, paper, pastels, watercolors, acrylics (whatever), and grace us with her creative gifts. Julie adds the following:

"A couple of valuable things I learned included how to not draw with lines and to abandon whatever (non-relevant) rules people think there should be. I am happiest when I apply this to my approach to life, and I am lucky to have married someone who embraces that. Now approaching 50, I am moving on from being a housewife with talent (a badge I have worn proudly). I am physically putting myself inside my workspace a lot more—it's completely right-brain stuff, and it's blissful. All I need is to get the music going again.

"I've discovered I am a bit of a late bloomer, or perhaps it is that I have managed to learn how to manage my depression better over my adult years. Five years ago, I learned to ski, two years ago I got my first driver's license. I have learned to put more trust in myself, that I won't let myself down.

"My dad has given me some good advice over the years. One is the secret to happiness. I will get to that later. Another is to surround yourself with good people. The latter is key—lottery win number two for me is having a tiny smattering of amazing people around the globe. I don't allow myself to wallow in loneliness when I consider the quality of my personal connections. I call them 'My People.'

"I have few regrets in life. There is no point in rehearsing what might have been. However, I do regret not ever becoming a pole dancer (admittedly, I never had the legs for it) and my rock-band, "The Weight Gains," hasn't really taken off, but we are going to be huge. Though I don't have any firm members yet, the band is absolutely thriving in my *head. I have a lot to say/scream in my lyrics because peri-menopause is the absolute perfect time to pick up a guitar and be a punker. I probably should learn a few riffs before I get further along. Oh, dad's secret to happiness? "Always have something to look forward to."*

Julie makes herself at home wherever she is, but more important, she makes everyone who knows and meets her, equally at home! She is a lady for all reasons and all seasons!

Husband, Debashis, summarizes his love or Julie briefly and eloquently:

"It is difficult to capture the many aspects of Julie, let alone write briefly what she means to me or my life. Perhaps, the briefest way is to say, Julie is the voice of reason, the beautiful companion, the arbiter of taste, the secret of my success, the artist in residence and the mother of my son. The list needs to be more complete, but it would be very, very long."

Inseparable

Speak to me of your peace, Jesus. Not our peace: tight, limiting—circumscribed by our wants and needs, while creation groans and we hear it not. 'From dust we came to dust we will return.' We ARE the earth betraying itself, euthanizing its wonder, choking its air, stripping its streams, insatiably obliterating sister creatures great and small—hell-bent to dance our dance and have it all. Speak to me of peace that doesn't sleep. Peace that multiplies joys and divides sorrows, peace that celebrates creation, peace at war with, separation, for to love one is to love all, and to wound one is to wound all.

Economy

Economy, conciseness, brevity. A trinity of redundancy. Let me try again, God. "Open my eyes, my ears, my heart. Guide my hands, my feet. Forgive. Forget. Revive. Release. Show me Your face in those I meet. I'll savor each step along the way and taste each drop of life this day!"

Appreciation

The "Thank you!" didn't come and I walked away, my small gift unacknowl-edged. A helping hand, a favor given, neither a mite nor a million—just a throw-away kindness tossed to the wind that deep down begged some return, some response. Nothing! No look, no nod, no smile.
My brief breeze of mutuality blown away, and something itches inside. Something missing that shouldn't be missing. To give and not get. Why should it matter? But that is the matter, isn't it? That which is truly given seeks no reward. P.S. If this makes any sense at all, "You are welcome!"

Wonder

Wonder opens windows, doors, pathways, and passages!
Its humble reverence hums softly in the night
   like silent shadow songs singing here and there
     its promise of déjà vu. That strange remembrance of something
     old, yet new, seeking to be explored, birthed, given air.
A confluence of what is, was, and what might be
   just beyond peripheries of knowing and not knowing.
Sleepless, stirring, never silent,
   wonder's sweet and bitter queries whisper in the wind.
On seas of possibility they float within the mind,
   impatient—unwilling to await some distant spring.
A spinning, swirling vortex of mystery that teases tepid faith:
"Go ahead. Peel it back! Take one tiny taste!"
Can you hear its call? Wonder's painful pilgrimage,
   to question and critique, to deconstruct and reconstruct,
   to fit in one more piece.
Jesus, Buddha, Shiva, Krishna—gods with many names.
Sacred rites, sacred sites, miracles and starry nights
   that birth a thousand Christs.
Fantasies and fallacies mapping out your life.
There's tragedy and majesty when dogma leaves the room,
   stale air dies, windows rise, and wailing walls come down.
Drops of truth in narratives, in metaphors, in poetry
   that paint beyond the lines with hints of life's sheer ecstasies
   that need not sing nor rhyme.
Each a joyful pondering—another hill to climb.
The dance goes on, and nothing seems the same
   —I'm holding on while letting go. while wonder calls my name.

Rehearsal's Resurrection[25]

Some doors should remain closed, God.
Yes, I know, this goes against trust, openness,
    and faith that even the darkest memories
    can be pierced by light and reconciliation.
So be it. But, the mantra that one must confront the dark to defeat it
    makes little sense when the enemy's disempowered
    and no longer permitted rehearsal's resurrection.
Get over it. Close the door. Nail it shut. Move on.
Isn't that what forgiveness is about?
There's something sad about enjoying poor spiritual health
    —opening the door again and again to past misfortunes.
Free me from the litany that showing my scars
    in the mirror of self-acknowledgment redeems me.
I am more than that. And so are you, God.
The horizon that calls is not behind me.
Past tragedies and sin have had their day.
And, yes, they've helped in their own strange way
    to pave my walk today.
So, let them be. Let them rest.
New possibilities await, straight ahead.
New doors—some good, some not so good.
No hesitation, no looking over my shoulder,
    grant me the courage to open them.

Reflection: Who You Are

It seems to me that religion is *who* you are not what you say you believe; it's what *you come alive to*. Religion (Latin: *"re-ligare"* meaning to re-connect) is the willingness to befriend creation, to be reunited to the sacredness of community in all its diverse expressions. The poet was right, "Death *is* the mother of beauty."[26] Life without limits is life without meaning. Each passing minute screams to be filled and squeezed out with no guarantee of another sweep of the second hand. Life cries to be lived fully in the *now*. To be 'born-again' is not to be baptized or born from 'above' so much as it is to be re-born by the Spirit each day so deeply that joy, hope, love, and peace spill out in all you say and do. Tomorrow is paradise postponed; healthy religion is a collective celebration of today's resurrection sunrise.

Somewhere In-Between
Kerry Lee Peters

If daughter, Kerry, felt disadvantaged as "the middle child," Penelope and I would be last to hear it. Correction, no one would hear it. Privacy and confidentiality are for Kerry, sacrosanct to a fault. Her 'Good Samaritan' qualities see her aiding friend and stranger at considerable self-sacrifice. Quick to meet other's needs, Kerry is reluctant to burden others with her own concerns. As self-appointed peacemaker between her two sisters she earned the nick-name, "Sister Veronica." In a sense, anyone perpetually helping others at undue cost to self, is a *middle child*—somewhere between finding a healthy balance as helper and being helped.

Kerry is not an attention seeker. Her avoidance of center stage is not due to shyness. She simply refuses to measure her achievements as particularly special or noteworthy. Micah's admonition,*"What does the Lord require of you but to do justice, and to love kindness and to walk humbly with your God?"* (Micah 6:8 NRSV) is at the heart of who she is.

Her desire to help others saw her return to school to earn a diploma as a child and youth worker, which birthed a twenty-year career as an educator. The past seventeen years she has served as an aboriginal support worker for elementary and secondary students, a job she excels at and loves. Here is part of her journey in her own words:

"I have had the privilege to grow and evolve in my years as an aboriginal educator. Starting out as a first nation's worker, I naively believed one could shape culture but soon learned that culture shaped me. The teachings of aboriginal elders, my students, their families, and the support of co-workers, awakened me to the unique needs of native children and youth. Something as simple, yet important, as not requiring troubled students to make eye contact quickly built trust and rapport.

"Challenged by kindergarten and grade one students with anger and truth telling issues, I searched for social skills resources with an aboriginal component without success, so I decided to create my own with the help of an aboriginal artist friend of mine, Annie Bock. My fingers hit the keyboard composing first nation children's stories with a passion and freedom I cannot fully describe. It has been fun developing my series, Aboriginal Coping Stories for Little Souls. Three books in the series have been well received by students, teachers, and superintendents: Tuwa the Turtle's Tummy Trouble, (learning to tell the truth). Putak the Polar Bear's Problem, (dealing with anger issues and problem solving) and Muk the Mouse's Miserable Day, (struggling with loneliness, humility, and making friends). Boefloe the Buffalo's Broken Heart, (coping with family separation and anxiety) is presently in draft form.

"These stories have not yet been published, however, they have been well used in the school setting and shared with my family and friends. I am exploring publishing possibilities. Nonetheless, I am grateful for the opportunity to have developed this useful resource that was inspired by my journey as an aboriginal educator. I tell my students, "Five years ago I never would have thought I would write an aboriginal children's story, so if I can fulfill a dream, you can too."

"I am passionate about my job whether it be in a classroom, group setting, one to one, or out in the community/reserves. It's an honor to support students and their families academically, socially, physically, mentally, and spiritually. Sometimes being a mentor and encourager is as simple as providing an alarm clock for a perpetually late secondary student. Other times it's at the cost of tears. The reward of seeing students succeed or graduate within an educational atmosphere that nowadays readily embraces their culture far outweighs the tears."

I am biased, of course, but Kerry does ordinary things in an extraordinary way. She is creative, compassionate, and supportive in her daily encounters with students and friends. Her pride and joy are her two adult children and four grandchildren. Simple things like a hello, a hug, a smile from a grandchild or a former student—give Kerry's life meaning. Sometimes it's as simple as the gift of an alarm clock.

God's YES!

*Each dawn births promises unfurled, whose gifts commence the daily dance
of choice and chance that shout God's "YES!" Wind and wave may hold at
bay new paths that chart Love's will and way and drown the Spirit's trust.
Yet faith runs deep beneath life's waves, a calm beneath the storm, a steadfast current of Love's stream, unending, ever strong. Fire and ice. Joy and
pain. Charge headlong into hope. Catch the wind within your sails, face the
maelstrom's scream—deny the dark its inky dream to rob your soul of sight.
Just beyond the bleakest night, dawns the day's delight. The sunrise of a newborn day, rainbow skies, seas of glass, a gentle breeze that comes your way
to greet the morning after. Another day to celebrate—another morn to smile
and say, "I'll strive to find Love's will and way and shout again, God's YES!"*

Let Us All Take Part

*Word power! Immense. Life-taking. Life-giving.
But then, you know that, God.
Let there be light—and there was light.
Let there be firmament—and there was firmament.
Let there be grass, and trees, and fruits,
    and all manner of crawling creatures—and there was.
And let there be discrimination and all manner of division
    and all manner of victims and segregation
    —and there was, there is, and will be.
And let us ALL take part. So, sad, we have.
So, sad, we do. So, sad, we will,
    so long as we give offense and take offense.
But, words can pull us together:
Words that make us, them—and them, us!
Words that harbor, help, and heal.
Words like friend, neighbor, sister and brother.
Words like forgive and forget, live and let live.
Words like unity, community, diversity, and harmony.
Words like joy, hope, love and peace,
    mutually given, mutually received
    and let us all take part.*

Wisdom and Compassion
Heather Lynn Moor

Our youngest daughter, Heather Lynn Moor, is religious. I can almost hear her say, "Ouch!" when she reads this. She is not religious in a lockstep, institutional, rigid theological sense, but in the only way true religion is measured—namely, by striving to live the right arrangement of relationships. Frankly, religion doesn't get any better than that. Heather's moral compass aligns with integrity, kindness, honesty, and compassionate judgment quick to call out inequities. She is comfortable in her own skin and doesn't hesitant to share her opinion and to speak up for people marginalized. Add to these qualities her joy for life, quick wit, bizarre humor, excellent writing and public speaking skills, and you discover a wonderful daughter, sister, mother, and wife who never settles for second-best in whatever she pursues. Too good to be true? A father's biased perspective? Perhaps, but those who know her would echo such accolades. Bottom line—Heather is anything but ordinary. She has a health and physical education degree from the University of Toronto.

Heather's work as activity director for a seniors' home provided her and its residence the greatest joy. She refuses to put people into categories prioritizing one above the other. Correction! She does place their family golden doodle, Bentley, slightly above others!

Heather's childhood was a blur of speed; agility; competitiveness; a zest for fun, life, liberty, and the pursuit of climbing. Whether clinging to a fire hydrant, scaling a tree, winning red-ribbon races, or defending her sister from schoolyard bullies, the only thing that slowed her was a depleted battery. Her mother and I found her atop our refrigerator when she was just a toddler. Don't ask. We have no idea.

When I emailed her a copy of her fire hydrant portrait at age eight, forty-eight-year old Heather duplicated the pose and replied with an update. Heather is a keen observer of life. She is highly sensitive to the needs of others and has intuitive common sense, counseling skills. She has been a godsend, particularly to her father since the death of her sister, Beth. Not an easy task while burdened with her own daily weight of loss. Thank God her mother's contribution to her DNA prevails over her father's. She is wise beyond her years, unafraid to face conflict, and a champion for the least, lost, and labeled. Hopefully, there's a little bit of me in there somewhere.

Wife to Bryce Moor (a wonderful son-in-law) and mother to daughter Kira, an honors graduate scientist of McMaster University, and son Braden, a gifted writer and "Nintendo master," Heather no longer climbs refrigerators, though fire hydrants are a piece of cake. She is highly competitive, and an avid sports fan complete with team hats, jerseys, and names and stats of players. Her father occasionally watches a football or baseball game. I don't know one player from another. Where did I go wrong? Nowhere! She and her mother are jocks! Her father's not—neither "now," "before," nor "after."

Reflection: Now, Before, and After

The journey from childhood to adulthood takes decades, but Einstein was on to something when he discovered time expands or contracts relative to circumstance. Touch a stovetop burner accidentally and a nanosecond becomes an eternity. Sit on a moonlit, park bench holding hands with "Ms. or Mr. Right" for hours and time loses measurement. I have heard forty-minute sermons that seemed like five minutes and five-minute homilies that have dragged on for hours.

I'm in my mid-seventies and in good health. Why do I think I still can run like a gazelle, move a fridge without breaking a sweat, throw a touchdown pass, score a goal, and dance until midnight? Bodies betray us. My "six-pack" is now a "one-pack," yet the me inside says I still am young, despite painful evidence to the contrary. Ego is a factor, but distorted self-deception is also a step-child of how we measure and experience "now." You are reading this sentence now, but it was "now" when I typed it. It is always *now*.

We self-minimize physical limitations brought on with age by substituting yesterday's strong, agile, vigorous *now* for today's *now*—a deception that can fuel aching backs, heart attacks, and premature death.

Walking forward into one's past can reap emotional concerns as well as physical. When we fail to put to rest poor decisions, hurtful memories, and lost opportunities, "what was" holds "what is" hostage. We find it easier to forgive others than to forgive ourselves. Give yourself a break! The Golden Rule, in this case reads, "Do unto *yourself* as you would do unto *others*." The past is the past. We can claim past misfortunes without them claiming us! In other words, let "before" tell its story stripped of guilt; fill "now" with new opportunities, and "after" will look after itself. In Jean-Pierre de Caussade's words, live "the sacrament of the present moment."[27]

Forgive and Forget

I see you, but do I see ME? Partly, "Through a glass darkly," as Paul
declares. Smoke and mirrors of self-acceptance cloud my introspection.
But this is not the sleight-of-hand of saccharine self-deception. I cannot hide
my shadow side, my secret sins, and silent cries. The scars of choice and
chance have carved deep tracks that do not wash away. Nor should they.
For acid tears no longer burn; they've left behind life's lessons learned, freed
now from guilt and yearning. Saint. Sinner. Slate wiped clean. Though
memory's scripts reside inside cancelled sin is not denied. Self-serving deeds
and deeds undone no longer scream my name. Power. Drained. Forgotten.
Wispy, shadowy scenes fade from view. I see them; they don't see me, ob-
scured by LOVE'S redeeming.

Floating Alone

Fingers. Keyboards. Monitors. The unread poet straining to say what can't be said. Pushing letters across a screen. Scattered. Over-worked. Redundant. No catchy phrases, no plot, no tailored thoughts. The clothes don't fit. Too loose. Too tight. Too taut. Typing stops. "WordPerfect" dies. No rhyme. No rhythm. No anecdotes or clever quotes. Stillborn prose dead before its birth. Shut it down. Rest in peace. Maybe tomorrow, the day after, next week? Somewhere, something floats alone, waiting to be born.

A Chance to Get It Right

Yesterday, for the first time, someone shouted, "It's a GIRL!"
*   someone looked love in the face and said, "I do,"*
*   someone took a first step—the game was muted*
*   and grandparents called.*
Yesterday, someone had their first kiss, received an "A" in spelling,
*   found rice in their bowl, a bed for the night.*
Yesterday, there were tears, joy, words of hope,
*   a friend's smile, a slate wiped clean,*
TODAY! Another resurrection morning—a chance to get it right!
*   Can we do it again tomorrow?*

Call Waiting

Pockets buzzing. Purses ringing. iPhones playing Mozart.
Available. Not available. Here. Not here.
In touch, yet out of touch. "Can you hear me now?"
Do you see me now? Should I wave for your attention?
Bluetooth heaven. Cell phone nirvana. Wireless paradise.
One-sided conversations. Private? Public?
Invasive. Intrusive. IRRITATING!
Strangers talking to themselves, hearing voices
*   I do not hear. No meds, no restraints.*
They're out there walking among us,
*   staring at screens, stepping into traffic,*
*   driving cars, buying groceries,*
*   eating lunch, doing the Zombie Jamboree.*
Their lights are on, but nobody's home. Hi-tech. No touch.
*   "I'm sorry, were you saying something?"*
*   A pain in your chest? Sorry, I've got to take this.*

I won't be a minute. Now, what were you saying?
   Push "3" for more options!
Remember when you were not available?
When a text message was a book, a magazine, a love letter?
When hands were not glued to ears?
When convenience was not an addiction?
When relationships were not measured by batteries
   and four bars of reception?
When being in touch WAS being in touch,
   holding a hand, seeing the color of their eyes,
   actually, knowing where you were,
   what you were doing, and whom you were with?
Something designed to bring us closer
   is driving us further apart, God. I'd finish this
   —but my pocket is buzzing!

Reflection: Containers of Truth

Stories are containers of truth. Stories need not be factually true to be profoundly true. Whether wrapped in a novel, parable or a fanciful movie plot, truth shines through. Renowned mythologist, Joseph Campbell, said, "Myth is what we call other people's religion." More to the point, myth is everyone's religion. Myth is the only wardrobe we have to clothe the ineffable in stories, written, said, sung and spun. It is a made-to-measure wardrobe that invariably never quite fits because its weavers cannot adequately tailor words to describe the indiscernible. In other words, myth is the language of metaphor; it is our only means to presumptively convey what cannot be adequately expressed. Myth and religion are inseparable.

Faith in a Box

"Sell your cleverness and buy bewilderment."
—Jamaluddin Rumi, 13th Century Sufi mystic

Faith in a box: contained, maintained, squeezed shut gasping for air, tightly wrapped in creedal wrap, no longer free to sing, to soar, to stretch its wings of hope and exploration. Mastered by belief—twenty-six letters, shaped and selected, spelling its fate in pithy, iffy phrases long in length but short on substance. Sealed! Secured! Held fast by minds made small through lessons learned, letters earned, and sayings sacrosanct. Hear their hollow echoes straining at credulity. These ancient holy unctions steeped in orthodoxy: rites, rules, requirements, worship and beliefs unchallenged, unquestioned dwarfing wonder's reach, domesticating its soul. No hills to climb—no dangling ambiguities to tease a mind now closed. Ah, to drink in bewilderment, and live again.

Always on The Run
Chau Smith

Chau Smith looks ordinary—a short, pleasant, bundle of ordinary. But there is far more to this remarkable Vietnamese senior than the smile that welcomes customers to Chau's Alterations and Dry Cleaning in Independence, Missouri.

I am not a close, personal friend of Mrs. Chau Smith. I was introduced to her by a mutual friend, Tom Mills. Before meeting Chau, I had decided not to include additional portraits and profiles to what was becoming a never-ending book. Five minutes with Chau and her story had to be shared.

Chau is amazing proof there are no "ordinary" people. Her amazing exploits were published in an article, "Meet the 70-Year-Old Runner Who Ran 7 Marathons on 7 Continents in 7 Days" by NBC journalist Melissa Hung.[28] Yes, you read that correctly: age seventy, seven marathons, seven days! How? By working all day, every day, weeks on end, while training in the dark of night—rain, wind, ice, and snow!

Chau ran marathons in Perth, Australia; Singapore; Cairo, Egypt; Amsterdam, Netherlands; Garden City, New York; Punta Arenas, Chile; and King George Island, Antarctica as part of a challenge called Triple 7 Quest, operated by *Marathon Adventures*, which planned the itinerary and logistics. Melissa Hung adds, "she ran them all wearing a pink pussycat hat." That gets my vote!

When US Senator Mitch McConnell invoked an obscure Senate rule to silence Elizabeth Warren from quoting Coretta Scott King in the Senate chamber, McConnell's nasty quip, "Nevertheless, she persisted," went viral and to his dismay became a rallying cry for women's rights. "Nevertheless, she persisted," is more than a phrase to Chau. It is Chau!

Chau has incarnated persistence. It is not Chau's unbelievable athletic achievements that distinguish her as an "extraordinary," ordinary person. It's the rest of her story, profiled by Terry Young in a 1994 edition of *The Independence Examiner* that overshadows her athletic feats as revealed in Young's article:

"Since her arrival to the United States in 1972, Chau's dream has been to unite her two brothers and two sisters and help them settle in Independence. She realized that dream, and a promise she made 25 years ago to her dying mother, in October, when the only sibling remaining in Vietnam, her brother Tran Dung, stepped off a plane and onto American soil.

"When I was 19 my mother died, and I never forget what she say," said Chau, the second-oldest child in a family of five. *"She say, 'You know, you all have to take care of each other. No one will love you like I love you.' Do we always take care of each other?*

Taking care of each other is now easier. After 15 years of effort and $30,000 in plane tickets, Chau for the first time celebrates Christmas with all her siblings as well as with 21members of their families she fought to bring from Vietnam."

Melissa Hung, NBC journalist, writes: "Chau helped her relatives to navigate jobs, school, and meetings in their new country during the day; at night, she worked long hours." Melissa Hung's profile of Chau is a good read of an exceptionally good person. Check it out at www.NBC.com. I love Hung's quote from Chau:

"I always try to train in my mind the good things. So, even when I'm really in pain, I'm able to think about something else positive," she said. *"So, you don't think about, 'Oh my god, it hurts so bad. I hope I don't offend anyone, but I'm a woman. I have daughters. I have a granddaughter. I run to represent the women,"* Smith said. *"I'm against any man, powerful man, who think they can do anything they want to women without our consent, without our permission."*[29]

While writing Chau's profile the *Independence Examiner* reported Chau, age 71, had added one more marathon and a micro-continent called Zealandia to her uncanny achievements. (Her total now is eight marathons in eight days in eight continents). In the article, journalist, Michael Smith quotes Chau, *"I just figured that I am not getting any younger. Even though the eighth continent is not officially recognized, I wanted to go ahead and do it."* *Chau estimates she's run more than 80 marathons in her lifetime.*

A Better Me

Today, I'll ponder who I am and who I strive to be. I'll make lists of white-hat dreams to vanquish everydayness: to stand taller, eat less, walk faster, worry less, look up not down, awake to freeze-framed feathered wings and star-filled pregnant nights. I'll cease to gulp each spinning hour but sip life's precious gift of time and taste its daily wonder. I will find a better me—at least, I will today.

For Goodness Sake!

"My, O my, what a good boy am I!" A favor done, a note of thanks, a helping hand, a wallet returned with nothing missing. That's it, of course. "Nothing missing!" Each good deed done without thinking. No weighing its value, no saying "Well done!"—no credits gained, no stars in my crown. Just being good for goodness sake. "My, O my, what a good boy am I!" Really?

Reflection: Betwixt and Between

"Theodicy, in its most common form, is an attempt to answer the question of why a good God permits the manifestation of evil. Some theodicies also address the evidential problem of evil by attempting to make the existence of an all-knowing, all-powerful and omni-benevolent God with the existence of evil and suffering in the world."[30]

Is a god stripped of omnipotence worth singing about? Are we expecting too much or too little of God? Perhaps, both. Logic whispers, *"The line separating theism and atheism is paper thin."* Take note theological liberals (message to self), it is one thing to applaud the death of a cosmic Santa Claus; it's another to vest reason and logic with its own brand of divinity. Certitude is theology's antagonist. Our ideas of God are *not* God. The niggling question is: "If one aborts supernatural theism what remains at the end of the day?" Answer: mystery—that which cannot be explained.

C. S. Song in *The Compassionate God* says we have been handed a "high-voltage God" and a "high-voltage theology" by our tradition.[31] We have posited infinite power as the primary and characteristic attribute of deity, but power alone does not resolve life's problems. God's primary attribute is love not power. God does not exit stage left when heartache wins; God weeps.

What if omnipotence is not boundless, unlimited power? What if omnipotence is contextual, (i.e., the full extent of power resident and presently available)? I can exhaust *all my strength* to achieve a challenging physical goal and fail to do so because the task exceeds "ALL" my power. Process theology (and "pan*en*theism") posits that existence (including God) is in process as you and I are in process. Rejection of omnipotence is not new.[32]

Theologian Douglas John Hall in *God and Human Suffering: An Exercise in The Theology of The Cross,* reminds us that integrative suffering (the suffering of *becoming*) is fundamental to life. We cannot grow or develop free of growing pains literally and metaphorically. Joy and sadness are co-dependent. Pain, anguish, heartache, and grief are love's invoice. We do have power to alleviate *disintegrated suffering* (e.g., humanity's inhumanity—war, violence, terrorism, etc.) while nature's deathly dance of wind, wave, fire, and rain claim no capricious author.[33] Our feet shuffle awkwardly across skepticism's dance floor unsure if life's music is serendipitous or divinely composed. I am not into "religious magic," nevertheless my heady, liberal theology would willingly give logic a day off should "mystery" spare a loved one from the brink of death.

Betwixt and between, we want it both ways—a god small enough to fit our intellectualizations and large enough to fill our yearnings. It seems we cannot live without a god of our making—a god, who invariably looks very much like us, fits the space we give it, and dances to our tune. Albert Einstein said, *"Two things are infinite: the universe and human stupidity; and I'm not sure about the universe."*[84] He went on to say, *"A little knowledge is a dangerous thing. So is a lot."*[85] Particularly when you think you know everything. If your God can't surprise you; your God is too small.

Crumbs

Crumbs. On your lap. You tie. Your blouse.
Under the table. On the rim of your plate
    swept up, cleaned up, picked up—one last tiny taste of splendor
    pinched between finger and thumb.
Crumbs. The cat's delight. The dog's desert.
Little "Savior" leftovers for a Canaanite woman.
Listen. She's trying to get your attention, Jesus.
    Why the harsh reply? A racial putdown?
    "Send her away" your friends say, "she's not one of us."
Red, yellow, black, white, tall, short, fat, thin
    dine at your table, Jesus—a motley mixture of saints
    and sinners silently seeking attention.
Crumbs of communion, dollops of wine.
On bended knee they wait your meal's sweet blessing
    where none are sent away. None? None?
Do you hear them? Do you see them?
Homes that have no tables. Homes that have no crumbs?
Beyond the chapel, stomachs ache, mothers weep and wait,
    while infant eyes slowly close, no more to wake.
Listen. Do you hear them, Jesus? NO, of course not!
We are your hands, your feet, your heart, your ears
    —and WE'RE not listening.

Love, Law and Order
Thomas and Nancy Mills

Some people become instant "lifelong friends." Such is the case with Nancy and Tom Mills. "Love, Law, and Order" applies equally to Tom and Nancy with emphasis on the word "Love," because true law, order, protection, and service are rooted in love. Nancy and Tom demonstrate their compassion for others daily. Theirs is a legacy of service, protection, and pastoral care void of fanfare or spotlight. They see a need and fill it.

For eleven years, Nancy served as dean of the School of Nursing (University of Missouri Kansas City). During her leadership it doubled enrollment, tripled the size of its faculty, increased the number of students from underrepresented populations, boosted federal grant receipts, and established an undergraduate program to award a bachelor's degree in nursing. Before retirement, she also served as interim vice chancellor for research. She interrupted retirement to be interim dean of UMKC School of Dentistry. I had to Google these achievements because Nancy never refers to her accomplishments or awards. Her leadership and management skills now are focused on her greatest challenge—keeping husband Tom under control.

Tom served thirty years in law enforcement retiring as deputy chief of the Kansas City, Missouri, Police Department. Googling information regarding

Tom's career is futile, which persuades me that he has not retired and is working undercover. Like Nancy, Tom is reticent to share his career achievements and awards. A great storyteller, he never takes center stage in the heroic and life-threatening (and yes, sometimes humorous) stories he reveals when pressed. I am sure his actions spared many lives, and his bravery and self-sacrificing acts have taken numerous criminals off the streets. I am not going to give up researching his exploits; that is, if he doesn't shoot me.

Though Tom has prevented many offenders from "going home," his congenial personality makes friends and strangers feel at home. Meet him on the street, drop into one of his favorite restaurants, sit beside him at a movie (wherever/whenever) and you will experience a warm, friendly, inquisitive introduction. No doubt a career that saw the seamier side of life also called for not-so-friendly introductions, but Tom is one of the most caring and compassionate persons I know. If you need help, Tom is the first to respond.

Tom and Nancy work quietly in the background, sharing a ministry of care and compassion in our congregation and far beyond it. They are aware that social, philosophical, and theological constructs become binding. Rules, regulations, and religious interpretations can take on a life of their own.

Awake to What You Fail to See

Awake to what you fail to see: bright feathered wings in symphony that sail on winds of harmony—an autumn's blaze, a winter's wake, the smile of God upon each face. We are but the dust of stars. We are the earth, the soil, the sky—we are creation's cry. Each sun-kissed morn that greets the day, a drop of rain, a bird's refrain, the very air we breathe—we are! Give thanks for all you cannot see: the hidden notes of harmony, where atoms dance and spin in place in endless depths of inner space. Each blade of grass, each grain of sand, this spinning globe on which we stand, each chance we take, each step we make—are gifts of God's amazing grace. EASTER is each morning's song that sings our sleeping souls awake.

Reflection: A More Pressing Claim

Quick to accuse the Pharisees of extremism, we are slow to see how subtly we mirror their perceived rigidity. (Actually, Pharisees were respected by first-century Jews). At times, we face ethical dilemmas where competing values cry for a decision. We live in a world of diverse understandings of what is right and wrong. What do we do when torn between "lawgiver and forgiver?" What is our response to Paul's words,"rightly divide the word of truth"? We do the best we can. We empathize, sympathize, prioritize, and sacrifice. One value is sacrificed for the greatest good. Someone said, *"Sacrifice is relinquishment of that which has value in lieu of that which has a higher, more pressing claim."* Love can soften law's harshest demands.

When Law and Love in Tension Lie[36]

When law and love in tension lie and walls prevent
*   our searching minds from seeking life's ennobling call*
*   to liberate each soul confined, sweep from our hearts*
*   inordinate care of self and place and statutes fair*
*   to sacrifice these lesser claims in lieu of one that bears God's name.*
When words and rules mandate our faith, and hold us fast
*   to subtle creeds that bind God's love, as well as ours,*
*   from reaching those who cry in need, enlarge our hearts,*
*   expand our dreams, release our grip on safety's chains*
*   so, we may dwell in sacred space where love is viewed in every face.*
Let law and love share equal place as partners of transforming grace
*   lest wanting words preempt the worth of those*
*   whom God has given birth to life that's not convention-tied*
*   or squelched by fellowship denied.*
Flood then our souls with new resolve to open doors where hurts
*   dissolve. Help us to read above the lines of tenets scribed*
*   to shape our walk and find God's words eclipsing ours*
*   with higher hopes and nobler talk.*
For love, the "alphabet of grace,"[37] spells the dream that every race
*   shall live in God's community, enriched by faith's diversity.*

Setting God Free

Before we speak, you listen. Before we call, you answer.
Before we seek, you find us. For we are in you, and you are in us
*   straining to be seen and heard in all we say and do.*
Let us set you free, God. Free from our wounded self-indulgence,
*   our dwarfed desires, our stilted sensitivities, our verdicts set in stone.*
How brash to think we are your feet, your hands, your voice,
*   your grace, your love for all that is.*
You have laid down silent dreams, and we must sing their waking songs.
Let us be your breaking dawn that stirs awake
*   love's healing hope oft' uttered yet undone.*
Let us see anew each creature's worth and dignity
*   aflame with grace and majesty held fast by Love's community*
*   where every soul has home.*
Let us lay down safety's chains that bind our tongues from speaking out
*   where fairness and equality are strangled by inequity*
*   and saying all that should be said remains unsaid for fear of losing face.*
May we arise renewed by grace defeating preservation's place

—the politics of self-deceit that justifies our sluggish feet
from answering Love's clear call.
Let us stand on higher ground and walk Love's path of peace.

Making God, Real

"How do you make God real?" Good question.
Have we made you too unreal, God—a cosmic omnipotent deity
that intervenes at a whim—three saved in a plane crash,
the home team's winning run, the rain stops, the grass dries
in time for our family picnic?
Meanwhile, suicide, genocide, and ethnic cleansing go unchecked.
Real or unreal? We make you real when we give you the invoice for the
good and not-so-good happening to and around us.
You become real in our blaming and our blessing.
We make you real with bread and wine,
with hymns sung, prayers uttered, and sermons preached.
Let's face it; it's an on-again, off-again reality.
You are real when we need you. Not so real when we don't,
SO, how do you make us real, God? Good question.
Your abiding presence isn't a matter of convenience. It's 24/7.
It's personal, persistent, consistent. And it doesn't get more real than that!

Reflection: The Birth and Death of Religion?

Generally, we celebrate births and mourn deaths but there are also untimely births and triumphant deaths. The demise of anything that diminishes zest for life, liberty, knowledge, wisdom, and wholesome inter-relationship with the cosmos is cause for celebration. Conversely, the birth of anything that inhibits living abundantly, loving wastefully, and drinking deeply from life's living waters is stillborn. The death of religious fundamentalism would be cause for celebration. Extreme religious literalism is at the heart of many social, moral, and armed conflicts we face today. More people have been tortured and killed in the name of god than for any other cause.

Whenever a religion, culture, nation or individual claims exclusive ownership of the one and only true God—a god who is unquestionably on their side, whose word is utterly holy and unchangeable and whose cause they serve at any cost, Tribal Religion raises it head. Bishop John Shelby Spong says, *"The marks of a Tribal God are easy to identify. A Tribal God always has a chosen people and the problem with a God who has a chosen people is that everybody who is not a part of the chosen people become God's unchosen people. And it's a very close line between being God's unchosen people and seeing yourself as God's rejected, and if you can convince yourself that God has rejected people who are your enemies then it's very easy for you to reject your enemies. That's part of Tribal Religion; a Tribal God hates everybody that the chosen people hate. That is why Tribal Religion takes on terror—the imposition of its will against other people."*[88]

Erudite Confession

Forgive our subtle arrogance, our controlled smiles, rolled eyes and deep sighs slighting those who do not see what we see, hear what we hear, and think what we think. Forgive our scholarly sainthood falsely lifting us to lofty heights of "we know best." Sweep from our psyche sure footedness on the slippery shoals of faith where only the elect run quickly, safely, securely, until we fall that is. Not a fall from grace but one of saving face when all we thought we knew was but a drop or two of truth—its ocean unexplored and waiting

Reflection: Willing to Break New Ground

Everyone should hear their names being called in the forgoing "Erudite Confession." Faith, doubt, knowledge, belief and spirituality are not synonymous nor are they the exclusive purview of institutionalized religion. Queries I raise regarding these issues are not new, but are generations, even centuries old, and have been debated by minds far superior to mine. My musings do not break new ground.

Liberals, conservatives, fundamentalists, agnostics, and atheists are correspondingly intelligent beings. Members of one ideological standpoint are not by subscription to that standpoint smarter than those subscribed to another. Any elitist perception that theological education by itself outranks persons whose views do not align with the disciplines of seminary academia is arrogant. Knowledge, accrued from years of study resulting in letters after one's name are to be valued, nevertheless no one formally or informally educated can exhaust the mystery of what is deemed holy. The intricacies of today's miraculous technology—text, pictures, videos coded into 'ones' and 'zeros' downloaded to an iPhone filled with 8 billion transistors—boggles my mind. I'll make no wager if a "Flux-capacitor" in a DeLorean will someday transmit Michael J. Fox's great-great-great-great grandchildren 'Back to the Future.' Regardless, my inability to intellectually grasp the wonders of developing technology, does not dampen my desire to better understand and use them.

The same rings true for faith and belief systems. Theology is always partial, inescapably subjective, and evolving. The willingness to break new ground (often at the cost of letting go of cherished ideas) is limited only by our courage to pursue what passionately stirs us, accompanied by a consistent dose of humility. There is far, far more we do not know than what we claim to know.

Taking a Stand
Miss Kaylee (Peters) Hanson

The phrase, taking a stand, elicits scenes of brave souls confronting injustice, but taking a stand can be as simple and profound as listening, supporting, and encouraging the youngest among us. Kaylee's portrait caused me to reflect on the moral impact we have on children.

Children relate to people they like and who like them—people who have taken time to single them out with a special hello, a listening ear, and a reassuring word. In times of difficulty children remember adults who have remembered them. The simplest act of kindness registers with young people. We need to be "living sanctuaries" for children, neither inflating nor minimizing their fears and failures. Regardless of how insignificant a child's issue may rank on an adult's scale of concern, it may be earth-shattering in the mind and heart of the child. The core relationship question young people ask is not "What do you believe?" or "How do I fix this?" but "Will you be there for me?" At this age, Miss Kaylee's focus is getting up when she's down. It also should be ours.

Ready, Set, GO!

She's up, then she's down, rolls around like a clown then giggles and wiggles and wipes away frowns. Laughing and crying, she never stops trying, her toes she's applying to learn how to stand. Over and over her tumbles repeat till quickly she stands and her first step's complete. Right foot, then left, with her face all aglow, tiny Miss Kaylee is READY, SET, GO!

Faith's Voice[39]

We hear your call to pursue peace
    —to embody within us principles of justice and grace.
You have placed the hope of Zion in our hands.
Hands unequal to the task. Hands too often
    holding fast to lesser things.
Like sand sifting through our fingers, we've seen peace
    seep silently away. Forgive the detours of our faith.
Put us once again on its path seeking ways to actualize
    equity and community.
Grant us courage to challenge all that frustrates hope.
Let faith's voice rise above the hymns we sing,
    prayers we pray, sermons we preach.
Let faith's voice be our voice strengthening the weak,
    defending the abused, encouraging the meek.
Let faith's voice echo God's many names.
May pew, prayer mat, mosque, and synagogue have equal voice
    to celebrate God's joy, hope, love, and peace
    till the language of the soul is mutually shared.

Reflection: Standing with and For

Compassion is one's measurement of fairness and injustice fueled by empathy—the capacity to understand and share the feelings of others. Their story becomes your story, their hurt, your hurt. It is not a one-dimensional response. Compassion has two sides—a soft side ("to stand WITH") and a firm side ("to stand FOR"). We stand with others when we listen, support, encourage, and try to meet their needs. We stand for others when we speak for those who cannot speak and stand for those who cannot stand. The spine of compassion's both sides is our sense of "moral authority."

Moral authority subverts self-serving, prudential judgments. It weighs facts, motives, mitigating factors, and fuels courage to act. Moral authority weds *"the spirit of the law"* to *"the letter of the law."* It seldom lacks alacrity; its voice shouts, "Do what is right and do it now!" Empathy's hands and feet respond when *ought to* becomes *must do.*

When inequity is blatantly obvious, we *discern* right from wrong, who stands to win, who stands to lose, and what action is necessary. The operative factor is "discernment." Knee-jerk reactions can create more problems than they solve. Life's circumstances are varied. Some are black and white. Others are gray and ambiguous and call for evaluation to avoid premature judgments. Standing *with* and *for* others is rooted in mutual well-being and recognition of humanity's oneness—the deep reality that you are me and I am you. That which unites us is far greater than that which divides us.

Forward or Backward?

It's hard to journey forward worshiping the past,
 convinced what WAS exceeds what IS,
 immune to what MAY be.
It's hard to dream of better days outshone by purer times,
 convinced that in some golden age God's kingdom was sublime.
Frozen in our walk, hostage to the past,
 dogma's creedal certitudes lie beyond our grasp.
God's dream of peace does not reside in times romanticized
 by notions of a day and sect made pure and fantasized.
We're called to scale new heights, to step beyond what's known
 —to travel paths that set souls free and spells God's many names
 —where sacraments are not invoked by prayer or bended knee,
 but rise within one's daily walk fueled by empathy.
Swirling spires, whirling dance, holy fires, lotus flowers,
 wailing walls and pentagrams—faith has no constraints!
It flows beyond our claims; it dwells not in the past;
 it leans toward hope's future, where all are one at last.

Hands, Feet, and Caring Hearts

Here they are God, many faces, many races dancing after
 a God, who refuses to stay in the chapel.
Young hearts, young hopes, young minds
 leapfrogging over yesterday's rules,
 pushing the envelope, searching for space,
 hungry for meaning, needing your grace.
Can you hear them, God? "What should I do? What career to pursue?
What courses to take, what companions to make?
Whether to marry and what to believe,
And are you for real, God—I mean, ARE YOU for real?
Is life just a rhythm, the music, the song
 an emotional high, a rush that's soon gone,

have I screwed-up the game before it's begun?"
So many questions, stirring inside,
teasing and testing, tried and untried
fumbling for answers escaping their grasp.
They need breathing lessons, God.
We all do. Not to make life easy, but worthwhile!
Breathe into them high hopes.
Let them stretch for what is best. Help them live life's questions,
unsatisfied with yesterday's answers
Grant them peace with what is and what it is not.
Wash away stilted desires. Help them dream BIG
fully awake, fully committed
—free to pursue new understandings,
free to try, fail, and try again.
Renew, them. Restore them. Make bare your love for them
through our hands, our feet, our listening ears
and caring hearts.

Faithful to the Vision[40]

God, grant us courage, lest we fail to meet the challenge of this hour for fear assails our trembling will when e'er we rest on our frail power. We must not wait nor hesitate to raze the walls that segregate that harden hearts and amputate the Peace of Christ, we incarnate. We are the hands and feet of peace. We are its voice that brings release to those whose lives are victimized by trends and rules that minimize. Speak now for those who cannot speak. Stand for those who cannot stand. The church cannot confine its faith to pulpits, pews, and temple spires. Swing wide its doors, create new paths where justice walks, and love inspires. Proclaim God's grace. Pursue God's peace. Confront the powers whose aims decrease zionic dreams through subtle schemes that use God's name for selfish means. Above all else be faithful to the vision grace has placed in you—to actualize God's dream of peace where unity and harmony are blessed by rich diversity—where love prevails, and no one stands alone. Let nothing sway us from the call to share hope's healing power.

Paradise postponed. The dream. The yearning.
The great hope that hope is not enough,
*   that somehow—above, beneath, beyond, within—*
*   the universe will speak at last its sacred name*
*   in every fragile soul and love will have its way.*
"The Peaceable Kingdom"
Here and now, not there and then!
No longer postponed.
No longer trapped in Godly-talk and honeyed phrases
*   filled with meaning, bereft of life.*
Paradise—freed from feathered angel wings,
*   dreamland ecstasies, and wispy mansions in the sky.*
Enslaved no more by onion-skin promises
*   held fast by literal Holy Writ.*
May new horizons stretch our hopes
*   and may we strain to reach them.*
A glimpse, a grasp, a fleeting tug to pull them home at last.
No longer cast beyond the pale.
God's dream alive postponed no more.
Set free beyond our yearning.

Reflection: The Whole Magazine

The Samaritan woman's encounter with Jesus at the well awakens us to live large and live well, to live spiritually without being religious. Without being religious? Dietrich Bonhoeffer is credited with the phrase "religionless Christianity"—a phrase that suggests that Jesus's chief mission was to destroy religion. The religion of his day was a religion of commandments of does and don'ts. Mainly don'ts. Depending on who does the counting Judaism in Jesus' day had 613 commandments: 365 negative ("Thou shalt not") and 248 positive ("Thou shalt"). Jesus was not a Christian. Jesus was a Jew and worshiped as a Jew. He demonstrated that life did not serve religion; religion served life. Any religion that judges and enslaves people by self-serving rules, and regulations strangles life.

Time Magazine occasionally features a 'Religion Page' reporting religious news and views. For people in Jesus day religion was the one page in their lives that provided salvific guarantee conditional, of course, upon their fulfilling its rules to the letter—whereas Jesus demonstrated religion was not a check list, not one page in life's magazine. It was the whole magazine. True religion is everything you say, everything you do, every minute, every day. It is life lived abundantly.

Living the Questions
Kenneth McLaughlin

Kenneth L. McLaughlin: chief executive officer, minister, hymn text author, charitable fund raiser, and lawyer is the ONLY person who required a signing bonus and payment in perpetuity for use of his likeness. The fifty-page indenture (witnessed by his wife, Suzanne, commissioner of oath) exacted a substantial payment in advance plus a percentage of book sale profits. (Insert smile). Why did I sign this? Net profit projections are iffy. Based on early lack of sales, Mr. McLaughlin owes me $37.17. (He is supposed to laugh when he reads this. He won't).

People who live life's questions are not merely inquisitive; they are driven to understand what makes things tick. Their curiosity is boundless and dissatisfied with pedestrian answers. They probe mysteries (great and small). I have never met anyone whose range of interests, general knowledge, and appetite for information is as insatiable as Ken's. Thank God, for Google.

Ken never hesitates to express an opinion regardless of fallout. He unabashedly pushes back against ideas and actions he deems unjust, unfair or nonsensical. His unadorned tell-it-like-is directness occasionally finds him "burning bridges in front of him" when his lawyer persona emerges, yet he can deftly span dissent with self-effacing humor.

Ken loves music, art, architecture, geography, and interior decorating. He is widely travelled, and prides himself on facts, figures and his knowledge of cities, countries and cultures. He is a gifted hymn writer, a self-taught pianist, and is an excellent teacher and public speaker. His quick wit and humor is perpetually peppered by willingness to laugh at himself. Ken informally mentors young adults—often taking them to lunch—listening, offering advice, encouraging. He spearheaded a major renovation of Walnut Garden's church facility, transforming its entrance aesthetically and providing access for physically challenged worshippers.

Enough! Ken is not flawless. To say more of his attributes verges on deification! (OK, just a one more—he is a skilled interior designer and decorates his home seasonally). As stated Ken's unvarnished directness can put him at odds with others albeit his motives are ideological not personal. He expects candid no-holds-barred meaningful debate. Ken's number one deficiency is Facebook addiction. His minute-by-minute posts garner responses, whether his topic probes the momentous or mundane. Each day countless friends are put on the witness stand wondering, "What can he possibly ask next?" I have dubbed him, "Mr. Post-It" Were he suddenly to cease and desist, Facebook might go under. Bottom line? Ken is the antithesis of "ordinary." Here is a guy whose myriad abilities are overshadowed by his response to those in need. His kindness is free of fanfare or notoriety. Not bad for a lawyer! Not bad for anyone.

Benevolence

Have we shaped and formed you? Dressed you in or dreams? Wrapped you our liturgies? Blamed you for our schemes? Placed you on a throne of grace? Put magic in your hands? Prayed to you to save our souls and knit our broken seams? Was one of you not good enough? Did we split you into three? Have we trapped you in our ancient creeds and faithful fantasies? Could it be you dwell in me and all the other ME's? That all that is resides in you, beyond our mental means? Could it be you're not our judge, a cosmic king or queen—an inconsistent Santa Claus we've never heard or seen? Forgive our strained theologies, our fact-filled strategies. We'll celebrate the mystery—the eternal flow of life, of death, of pain, of joy—your presence oft discerned, a push toward benevolence beyond our wildest dreams.

Blocked

A blinking cursor. A cold computer monitor waiting for a keystroke, a letter, a word, a string of thoughts. Fingers frozen. Stoic. Hesitant. Blocked. Waiting for something—anything. A word, a phrase, a new thought painted by the mind—pushed to the surface saying what cannot be said. So, concise. So, poetic. So, simple. Quick. Terse. Truth unwrapped economically bubbling with the heart's surprise, "Yes! Yes! Why couldn't I have said that?" I can't.

Peeking Inside

Every so often, it's time to fess up. To peel back the layers to get at the core of who I am. Occasionally, I summon enough courage to scrape away self-veneer and peek inside. It's not fun. I don't always like what I see, which is disconcerting because basically, I like me. It's not a matter of judgment day or scratching the surface for some shadowy hidden truth, God. And it's not a game. It's not hide-and-seek. For the most part, I have a handle on my gifts, graces, failures, and flaws. I know black from white, God. It's the grays of life that challenge me—because that's where morality lives.

What If?

What if we had a war, and nobody came?
What if bombs were smart enough to simply stay at home?
What if friendly fire was scattered flesh and bone
   —yours and mine, not them and theirs, someone close to home?
What if neatly folded flags were never widow's gifts?
What if presidents and kings on front lines took a shift?
What if troops were never sent to even up a score
   and hurriedly brought home again when "votes" are valued more?
What if deep within the heart of every foreign friend
   there is no US citizen striving to be freed?
What if they have better ways and we're the ones in need?
What if kings, and queens, and parliaments outshine
   the Stars and Stripes, and freedom thrives
   in governments of many different types?
What if war was no more—if diplomacy was love
   —if hope was dressed in kindness and peace was not a dove,
   but lived within relationships blessed in mutual love?
What if vengeance could not live in lives made large by fame
   and leaders told the truth instead of playing games.
What if strength was gentleness, if diversity was blessed,
   if power found vitality when weakness was confessed?
What if every note we sing declared each soul has worth
   that every heartbeat is the same and hungers for rebirth?
AND WHAT IF, we declared, "World Peace!" and everybody came?

Little Questions

It's the little questions that bother me.
Why traffic lights are ALWAYS RED.
Why they're SO long—mocking my need for speed
      when my only deadline is me.
Why the phone rings when I don't want it to?
Why letting go is so hard when deep down
      I know I've hung on too long? Why I say no,
      when I should say yes—and yes, when I should say no?
Little questions. Little disturbances loom like elephants,
      turn my face red, my knuckles white, my disposition sour.
Never mind the mysteries of the universe,
      eschatology, and world peace.
Forget about drought, famine, terrorism,
      tsunamis, and power politics.
There's a red light staring at me—JUST ME.
Me in my small corner that's bigger than the world.
What red lights put you on hold, God?
What prayers go to voicemail?
Never mind angels' wings, parting seas,
      commandments carved in stone.
What are your little questions?
      "When will love have its way?
      When will sunsets be seen, and birds heard?
      When will smiles outnumber frowns
          and friends outnumber enemies?
      When will they *become* us *and* thee *become* me?*"
But, these are not little questions—are they?

Freeing Jesus

Is there room for awe and wonder when faith and facts collide?
Can the cracks in creed's cathedral let the light of doubt inside?
Is our dance of orthodoxy plagued by rhythms petrified?
Can we hear within God's music Holy cadence that's denied?
Is there room for minds to question? Must we follow in lockstep?
Is the Jesus that we follow trapped within our frozen texts?
Can we free him from our making and our shaping and our sects?
Can the Love of Jesus claim us, unconfined by creedal scripts?
Is the "Peace of Christ" a slogan said and sung to satisfy?
Is its hope beyond achieving in a world where millions cry

for a faith "alive" and "breathing" that mere words cannot supply?
Can we sing sweet songs to Jesus when our faith is unapplied?
Can we spell the gospel story with our lives as "living words?"
Can we offer hope and healing with a faith that is deferred?
Can we celebrate all names of God with grace that is denied?
Let us free the peace of Jesus from the ink of faith defined.

Reflection: Breathing Room

It seems to me Jesus must be very tired. Tired of carrying the burden of your sin and mine. Tired of prayers tagged with his name, of hymns and saccharine love songs, and blessings pronounced over a last name that wasn't his. Tired of being part of a Trinity he never heard of. It seems to me that in between parables and miracles, he had stomach aches, mosquito bites, disagreements with his friends, enjoyed his favorite foods, had irritating habits, and had little adoration for his critics. It seems to me he didn't smile all the time, lost his temper, and shook his head when he was misquoted. Sound familiar? It seems to me, he was very, very, much like you and me. Nevertheless, no other has demonstrated so powerfully what it is to be divine and human by reminding us that we too are divine and human. Not permitted to be a man for his season, we have made him a man for all reasons—a prophet who broke the cultural, political, theological, shackles of his day—a rebellious carpenter's son who championed the least, the lost and the labeled—a man worthy of discipleship who gave all he could give to free the captives and who in turn became captive to magical and holy accretions we have laid upon him. Who could not be claimed by such a man? I for one am. Unequivocally! Maybe we need to remove some of the weight we've heaped upon him, carry it ourselves, and give him a little breathing room. After all, it seems, to me, it would be the Christian thing to do.

All or Nothing

Dot each "I," cross each "t," each word and verse of holy writ
that marks life's tune with measured notes
held fast by we who play them.
"All or nothing" is the game, a packaged faith where truth is named
by rhythms fixed unchanging.
A deathly sleep of worshiped "facts" that segregate and foster hate
and close the mind's awakening.
A maddening mien of certainty
secured by literal recipes with sacred tomes off purity
—where lines are drawn; walls are raised; and wars are waged
with holy flags by they who see the face of God
reflected in their own.

Nevertheless, She Persisted
Suzanne Trewhitt McLaughlin

Suzanne Trewhitt McLaughlin has a string of university degrees, including accounting, master of divinity, and doctor of ministry degrees. She should have an honorary doctorate in cooking and another in "advanced selective hearing." Suzanne has mastered a unique, self-defense, ability to block out husband Ken's non-stop humming, whistling, talking, singing, and onslaught of perpetual queries. When pushed to "the max" she lovingly responds, "ENOUGH Ken!"

On a more serious note, Sue's accomplishments and talents are myriad. She has served in various leadership and management positions: accountant and financial analyst, minister, seminary instructor, and associate dean of Community of Christ Seminary and Saint Paul School of Theology.

Her portrait title, "Crafty Lady," is inspired by Sue's amazing ability to create fun crafts with her grandchildren. She loves to knit and excels at cooking, which pays delicious dividends to Ken and all who sample her epicurean delights. Sue actively applies late feminist theologian, Nell Morton's concept, "Hearing into Speech."

We empower one another by hearing the other to speech. We empower the disinherited, the outsider, as we are able to hear them name in their own way their own oppression and suffering. In turn, we are empowered as we can put ourselves in a position to be heard by the disinherited (in this case other women) to speaking our own feeling of being caught and trapped. Hearing in this sense can break through political and social structures and image a new system. A great ear at the heart of the universe—at the heart of our common life—hearing human beings to speech—to our own speech.—Nell Morton[42]

Sue provides a sense of safety and shared personal "sanctuary" where others are empowered to express deeply held feelings often voiced for the first time. But hearing into speech is not exclusively a group and individual personal relationship. Sue organized a successful chapter of "Dining for Women,"—a charitable program in which women meet monthly to share a potluck meal and donate funds to help disadvantaged women and children in developing countries. In this sense, "hearing into speech" is transformative for friend and stranger as close as next door or physically and culturally worlds apart.

It's Not Enough[43]

It's not enough to kneel in prayer and share in wine and bread.
It's not enough to give our tithes when children go unfed.
It's not enough to sing God's praise and bow our heads in prayer.
It's not enough to preach from texts when wanting souls despair.
It's not enough to speak of faith with words and creeds extreme.
The time has come to demonstrate faith that lives God's dream.

Peace Comes Alive

The Peace we seek is not enslaved by cultural points of view
*   nor does it dwell in lofty scripts and creeds concretized as true.*
Peace comes alive in you and me in all we say and do
*   to live the meaning of God's grace restoring life anew.*

When Faith and Disbelief Collide

When faith and disbelief collide, we dare not sweep doubt's gift aside
*   for probing questions stir the mind and open doors where truths abide.*
Clinging to and letting go, doubt's dance of pain and joy unfolds
*   when ancient creeds and blind belief release their grip and stranglehold.*
A steppingstone to higher ground, doubt frees our captive litanies:
*   the hymns we sing, the prayers we pray,*
*   the lessons learned, and homilies are not the works of certainty*
*   but humbly frame faith's mysteries with wanting words*
*   too weak to name God's dream for Love's community.*

We cannot find simplicity this side of life's complexity
    with faith confined by dogma's dark duplicity.
With searching minds to probe life's depths,
    with trust and hope no longer blind,
    a faith that's true at any cost, will paint beyond the lines.

Winds of Change

Winds of change stir every age and cannot be restrained
    nor can the maps we've drawn of God—divinity contain.
Our wanting words, our treasured texts, our tenets firmly claimed
    cannot hold fast within their grasp a God of many names.
Change sets us free from certitude; it breaks down creedal doors;
    it steps beyond constrained beliefs, horizons to explore.
Make no mistake, the winds of change are never meek nor mild;
    they storm the soul, coil the mind, disturb faith's sleeping child.
They sweep aside self-certainty. They question your identity
    and all you hold as true. They pierce the heart and wrench the soul
    for what you believe is who you are—that which says you're whole.
Salvation seeks no distant shore where judgment measures
    who you'll be just beyond death's door.
Salvation happens here and now—God's breeze of transformation.

Scales Dispersed

When shimmering stars in inky skies no longer sing their splendor,
When dimpled hands and natal eyes no longer stir birth's wonder,
When green's not seen and golden beams of sunlit streams
    hide beneath the day's routine,
    the here and now of heaven's face is lost to grace
    and we who sing a savior's song, sing but the words
    and fail to live their meaning.
A moment's pause to drink life in, to stop, to look, and listen,
    to see beyond the rush and rhyme, the daily grind
    that mutes the sounds of angels' wings
    and clouds our murky vision.
Let the Spirit breathe anew,
    let its whisper rise in you—its chorus of confession
    of all that's bright and beautiful, birthed within the usual.
A second look. The scales dispersed—the spirit's sweet awakening.

Let Us Be Your Amen[44]

Compassionate God, who weeps for the poor and wounded,
forgive our self-absorption—our penchant to circumscribe life
with needs and self-comfort at its center.
Open our ears to the lost, the least, the labeled.
Let their tears be our tears, their hopes our hopes,
their fears our fears.
Count us among the displaced, diseased, mistreated.
Not in word only, but in willful acts of love magnified by grace.
We are one with your creation, God,
yet we have ravaged its beauty by wanton consumption.
May we heal its wounds for its wounds are our wounds,
and our wounds are your wounds.
Let this prayer come alive in us. Let it speak loudly.
Let us be your "amen"—the "so be it" of who we are
and who you are calling us to be.

Reflection: Faith Unfinished

A people open to revelation's transforming voice must be willing to be surprised. If God cannot surprise you, then your God is too small. Despite a stormy history that has seen us cling to then let go of one cherished understanding after another, we must not stay the course of theological exploration. "The Truth must dazzle gradually," writes Emily Dickinson, "or every man be blind."[45] The motto inscribed on the library at Virginia Theological Seminary, describes a healthy sacred journey, "Seek the truth; come whence it may, lead where it will, cost what it may."

We cannot sing with integrity, *"We limit not the truth of God to our poor reach or mind"* or the chorus, *"The Lord hath yet more light and truth to break forth from his word"*[46] if our best understandings are couched in beliefs and practices that have no breathing room. We must remain open to inspired counsel. A faith not in ferment is not faith at all. Ours should be a faith on the move—a faith that beckons us beyond where we are, to dream new dreams, to hope new hopes, to be Christ's community in daring and uncomfortable ways. We are called to go deeper—to mine greater understandings of discipleship and to do so unafraid—trusting that God's Spirit will shape and bless us by the very name we claim and that claims us: Christ, Jesus!

Beyond Duty
Cheryll and Tom Peterman

The first word that comes to mind when I think of Tom and Cheryll Peterman is "nice." Sadly, nice has lost its potency. It is overworked, or more accurately under worked. Nice suffers from the wishy-washy connotation that something or someone is merely acceptable. Nice jumps into my mind regarding Cheryll and Tom because they are not satisfactory; they are EXEMPLARY! Tom and Cheryll's care for others is constant, unassuming and sacrificial. "Nice," in their case, does not denote acceptable performance or likability; it reflects their overriding spirit of generosity in compassionately serving others. If pressed to choose another one-word description of Tom and Cheryll—faithful, considerate, kind, dependable, giving, and gracious apply, but "steadfast" rises to the top. For decades, they have volunteered for challenging church and community leadership roles. These responsibilities have not been free of frustration and significant personal cost. Despite such demands, Tom and Cheryll modestly focus on the plus side of the ledger declaring they have received more than they have given.

People who are steadfast do their duty, but duty is an uneasy, disturbing word. The Rev. Dr. Maurice Boyd in a sermon preached at Metropolitan United Church of Canada in London, Ontario, suggested that duty is a word that constantly expands it meaning. Duty is a work-to-rule activity—a measured response fulfilling an obligation or required expectation. Boyd would say, *"When you have done your duty, you know you could have done more."*

Duty is missing from their vocabulary. Never eager for the limelight, Cheryll's and Tom's service to others consistently exceeds what is expected. The bottom line? People who are steadfast go beyond duty. Theirs is not a measured response that gets them off the hook. They are hooked on their desire to do unto others as they would have others do unto them. For the most part, people who go beyond duty are *NICE*. Tom and Cheryll are! I am blessed to call them friends.

Hope's Song

In every breath of spring, new life is begun.
In every drop of rain, there shines a thousand suns.
In every starless night, there's promise of the dawn.
In sunshine and in storm—hope still sings it song.
Its melody plays on, birthed beyond your tongue
*   in promises made and steps tread.*
It finds its way in simple acts of love each day
*   —a card, a note, a helping hand, a listening ear, a newfound friend.*
Every soul has cracks within where joy, and love, and peace
*   seep in, where light abounds, and faith contends,*
*   assuring darkness will not win and LIFE'S sweet song is sung again.*

Living Your Part

"Let's live our part in the feast" says Paul, "not as raised bread
*   but flat bread—simple, genuine, unpretentious."*
Doesn't sound too appetizing, does it? Flat bread. Unleavened.
Uneaten? Not the main dish—something pushed aside
*   the palette wouldn't miss?*
Hardly! A little salt, pepper, a dash of spice,
*   a slice of bread (flat or otherwise) livens up the dullest meal.*
Each ingredient willing to be what it is! No competition.
No first or second place. Each adding its unique
*   color, accent, and pinch of flavor to the whole.*
Each alive, "living" its part. If only we could settle for that, God.
If we could just live our part and let everyone live theirs
*   my, my, what a feast it would be.*

Faithful Presence

When the path lacks clear direction, when night yawns from lack of light
*   and each voice screams for attention, what brings dawn to endless night?*
Tis the Spirit's faithful presence standing fast through night and day,
*   sowing trust amid the shadows step by step to show the way.*
When your dreams are scattered ashes, when hope seems torn apart,
*   and faith falters from life's clashes, what brings healing to the heart?*
Tis the Spirit's constant whisper weaving hope within your soul,
*   knitting fragile faith together thread by thread to make you whole.*
When each face is blurred by traffic, when your soul seeks sacred space,
*   and the press and pace rob family what fills life with saving grace?*
Tis the Spirit's faithful presence pouring peace upon your soul,
*   draining doubt of its tomorrow, welling up to make you whole.*
When you gaze upon a sunrise or hear a robin sing,
*   when the colors of creation paint the darkest night with spring.*
Tis the Spirit's joyful heartbeat here and now that makes you whole
*   rolling stones from lives lived empty, resurrecting every soul.*

Wise Befriending

Wrinkled hands, weathered face etched by pain and laughter.
Milky eyes no longer bright that squint and search
*   a thousand suns and moonless nights*
*   for memories of childhood games and fantasies*
*   where tireless days snatched victories*
*   in flights that saved humanity from narrowed understandings.*
Here beats an ancient hero's heart,
*   a measured mind no more confined to stilted comprehensions,*
*   set free to dream the dreamer's dream to soar above realities*
*   that choke life's full dimensions. Youth's vigorous prize lies fast asleep*
*   buried deep in summer days unending,*
*   yet finds reprise in stories shared in laughter's light*
*   illumined by seasons' telling.*
Give ear to what is said and felt, give time its wise befriending,
*   for aged beauty begs no shape, no size, no fleet of foot,*
*   no fashion wise, no compromise to gain the crowd's accepting.*
Look deep within these treasured souls
*   whose halting gait once scaled life's highest blessings.*
For they have walked where you have not and hold the keys to mysteries
*   that soon you will be seeking.*

I Think I Saw You

I think I saw you today. I didn't say hello. I should have. Deep, dark chocolate eyes shining with wonder drinking life in, swallowing me and everything around you. Taking me in with that fleeting glimpse, that toddler's grin and giggle. I should have said hello.

I think I saw you today. Rushing at the light. Late for that meeting. That PowerPoint presentation painting your career. Run. Run. Run. Nice suit. Nice tie. I should have said hello. I think I saw you today. You've put on weight. Snug uniform. Tight. Confining. A frantic wave! Sign raised! Traffic stopped. Children safely crossing. Was it really you? I should have said hello.

I think I saw you today—dressed in black and dusty grey. Thinning hair. Paper skin. Cane and wheels for feet. Laughing with children playing in the park. Hungering for a smile, you paused and waved. I should have said hello.

I think I saw you today—wrapped in drops of rain, clothed in blades of grass and sun-kissed clouds—a sizzling orb of flame drowning deep at dusk. I heard you sing today—whispering in the wind, chirping feathered melodies, buzzing by some flowers. You held me up today, sustained my gait, gave me life and daily breath. I should have said hello.

Got up late today. Showered. Shaved. Same mirror—same face staring back. I don't think I saw you I should have. I should have said, "Hello!" "Have a nice day—let's LIVE it together."

Other Ways

You are NOT for sale, God. Nor is our holy bias. Let, instead, your peace breathe in us. Let it be what we say and do. Let it vanquish assurance that "our way" is the ONLY way. May we embrace your many names and faces— your whirling dance, prayer mat praise, saffron robes, and candle flames. The sacraments of life's JOY—different, diverse, authentic. Too often, Lord, ours is an everydayness discipleship stripped clean of joyful witness. We drown ourselves in tasks deemed holy—plans, programs, meetings. May they cease to bind us. May they serve, not be served. Help us seize each day with new resolve to speak hope to the hopeless, love to the loveless, joy to the joyless. May we, so richly blessed, bless friend and stranger with the living grace of your peace. May we, so impoverished receive grace from others— for ours is not the ONLY way.

Ɬumor, Enthusiasm, Compassion
Brian McMurray

I didn't intend to include Brian McMurray. I don't like him (SMILE)! His quick wit, off-the-wall humor, creativity, intelligence, problem-solving acumen, upbeat attitude, high-tech skills, and downright friendliness are turn-offs for the less gifted. (SMILE). Admittedly, he does not flaunt his abilities (please include acute "humility" as another reason to dislike him). Unlike the preceding "corny" comments, Brian's portrait title, "Cornguy," is not derisive. He is president, vice-president, chief financial officer, layout artist, web designer, film director, and janitor for "Cornguy Productions" (his own business enterprise).

Brian's primary career is creative director at OPUS Communications of Kansas City—a video and web client service where Brian's artistic, technical, and production skills are central to Opus's success. Brian is the director of product development and creator of "Church Updates"—a unique software program that is changing the face of ministry for several denominations. "Church Updates" has developed into a major Opus Internet service through which congregations communicate current news, happenings, requests for volunteers, and prayer support for members and friends. End of promo! No more crass promotion of products and services (please note: my previous books may still be available published under *Herald Publishing House* imprint).

Brian has captured the maternal affections of my wife, Penelope, which are supposed to be reserved for our daughters and, on occasion, me! Brian and Penelope have Facebook dialogues on myriad topics. Why do I put up with this? I have an iPhone, iPad, MacBook Pro, and an Apple TV. Things go wrong. Brian is an Apple expert. Do the math. Besides, two can play this Facebook game. I'm going to start exchanging recipes with his wife, Lyda, a multi-media-certified elementary teacher, who is equally intelligent, talented, and much better looking than Brian!

The bottom line is I am privileged to count this bright young man as a friend. Decades separate us but occasionally I see little bits of myself in Brian (wishful thinking on my part). Brian is more than a witty guy whose satirical and bizarre humor cracks up all who know him. He is a dedicated, caring husband and father who sips imaginary tea hosted by two young princesses, rolls on the floor with them, swims with them when they decide to be mermaids, and endures endless replays of Disney songs and videos. There is no second-best with Brian. It's first class all the way at the office desk, on the playing field, organizing a major church community event or helping those in need. Does he have faults? You bet (hidden somewhere). I am sure his wife Lyda could name a few, but from my experience, there is just so much day-to-day good stuff spilling out of this guy, they seldom squeak to the surface.

Where God, IS

Don't look up. Look around. Look at NICU babies, wrinkled skin, varicose veins, baggy eyes, whimpering sighs, gray hair, no hair, blinding smiles, and bleeding gums. Don't look up. Look around: faces at the diner, buffet banquets, tear-stained bowls. No room at the Inn? Sure, there is. Lots of room. Hotels, motels, castles, cardboard shacks, high-rise penthouses—brothel, bar and pew. Fat, thin, colored skin, cancer's ticking clock, wheels for feet and dancing toes. Birth, death, heaven, hell, all that's in between—peak of victory, dark night of the soul, good news, bad news, joy, grief, howling storm, stasis, silence, solitude. Here. There. Deep inside and stirring—there is no place where God is not.

Silent War

A silent war proceeds unchecked, unnoticed, unabated. Field, forest, mountain streams, creatures great and small. Nature drained to fill our needs, till nothing lives at all. Make peace with sand, soil, air, and sea, for they are you, and they are me. My wounds are yours—your wounds are mine. Ocean-deep, ocean-wide, we are one, and we reside within this silent symphony. Let God's rhapsody of peace resound anew with all we are and all we pray to be.

LYDA McMURRAY:

"Brian is the man of my dreams. When you first meet Brian, you immediately are drawn to his quick wit and sense of humor. I am always asked if I spend my days as his wife laughing, and the truth is that, yes, my days are full of joy and laughter with him by my side. In addition, Brian is hard-working, passionate, incredibly intelligent and creative. He often can see solutions to problems and brainstorm big ideas. Brian also cares deeply for other people. He has a compassionate heart and wants to make a difference for others wherever he can. I always see him helping others in their technology troubles, typing quick notes of encouragement to friends near and far, and physically lending a hand where help is needed. "For our two daughters, he is a dad who brings joy and laughter into their lives every day. He loves them fiercely, plays with them regularly, encourages and supports them in everything they do, and treats them as respected individuals. As a husband, Brian daily contributes to our household needs–often cooking meals, cleaning, and doing laundry as well as paying bills and dealing with home-maintenance issues. Whenever I've had dreams to be a stay-at-home mom, go back to school, or return to a career in teaching he has supported me in every way. Traveling to new places is my favorite way to spend time with him. We can talk for hours because he is and always has been my best friend. Each day I fall in love with him all over again because of the amazing person that he is. When I was a girl and dreamed of meeting the perfect boy, I never realized I'd be so lucky to actually find him. Brian truly is the man of my dreams."

A Second Look

Democrat. Republican. Born-again Christian. Atheist. Agnostic. Humanist. Gay. Lesbian. Bisexual. Straight. Transgender. Non-binary. Pansexual. Ball caps, Burqas, turbans, three-piece suits. What have I missed? Oh, yes, skin color, kinky hair, size, shape and culture. Look again! It's your neighbor: physicist, teacher, laborer, cop, the kid sacking groceries, the senior feeding pigeons, a face in the crowd. A million shades and sizes. Short. Tall. Thick. Thin. Plain Janes and Charlies. Names we can't pronounce. It's you and me. Wind swept. Rain-drenched, sunburned, sad-eyed, glad-eyed, worlds apart,

yet more the same than different. We laugh, we cry, we live, we die, we share
the joy of "being." You, me and all the other ME's. Labels be damned! Take
a second look—somewhere you'll see yourself looking back.

Labels

Imported. Exported. How many people can you be? Father, mother, sister,
brother, worker, team-mate, friend. And what about Jesus? Who wrote the
script? One name? Many names: Yeshua, Jesus, Bright Morning Star, Prince
of Peace, Emmanuel, Savior, Only Begotten, Lamb of God, Holy One.
"Jesus"—a name in everybody's game, blessed, cursed, ignored or forgotten.
"Jesus"—bandied back and forth with dressed up and dressed down expecta-
tions. Would he answer if you called him? Would he recognize his name? Can
he sort through all the labels, the magic and the fame? Can a carpenter from
Nazareth roll stones of doubt away? Can he rise in us and live in us? Do we
share his many names: HOPE for the hopeless, JOY for the joyless, LOVE
for the loveless, PEACE for all of God's faces? We greet them every day.

Rounding Off

Is this a round day or square day, God? Maybe I can round off some of its
edges, make things smoother? Round days are packed full of the good and
not so good with the good winning—or at least pretending to win. Pretending
to win isn't always bad. I'm not talking about Pollyannaish denial. All the
sincerity of a coat-hanger smile. Pretending isn't burying your head in the
sand. Pretending is joy's precursor—a willingness to say, "Sure, that's
miserable. It hurts. I wish it didn't happen but maybe its edges are not as
sharp as I think they are." Life is full of prickly things! They don't go away.
Nor should they! But maybe, just maybe if "I act as if"— if I pretend it's not
so bad, I can round things off a little, just enough to take the sting away. Are
your days round or square, God? Don't bother to answer, I think I know. We
ARE your days. Can you round us off a little?

Priceless

The following touches on theology's "scandal of the particularity" (resistance to the idea that
God would enter human history in a localized way—particularly the belief that Jesus is the
only way to God). Theologian Richard Rohr said, "A good poet tries to lead you into the
universal experience by leading you into the shock of a particular experience,"[47]

There are searching souls whose songs of doubt no choir ever sings
*   who sit in silent sanctity and wonder why they dwell therein*
*   where hymns of praise and homilies reflecting God's infinity*

leaves little room for questioning the magic it declares.
Fish to feed five thousand? Strolls across the sea?
Emptied tombs, feathered wings, stable stars, angelic choirs,
    a contradicting trinity where three are one and one is three,
    where someone pays atonement fees to free our souls from sin?
What of love for love's OWN sake—of grace that bids NO PRICE?
Redemption stripped of bargaining. No ransom on a tree.
No points to earn. No crown of jewels. No pit to dwell therein.
No rites to please. No this for that.
Just THIS: One who loved the least, the lost—never counting cost,
    who supped with sinners, scribbled in the sand,
    sent a victim on her way, touched a leper's hand.
One who wept at death, stood mute before "the man,"
    incarnated charity, leveled heights of hierarchy, accepted all with equity.
    —all for LOVE'S own sake. Atonement? The invoice never came.

Of a Dance Decided

Come sing with me; I have the words.
They're mine, their yours, their anyone's,
    who'll promise not to change them!
We've composed a perfect score of a dance decided;
    each pirouette, each sliding step, the rise, the fall,
    adagio, rehearsed in certitude and safety.
We swing and sway to melodies spun by ancient deities
    designed to fill our wants and needs
    and guaranteed redemption.
We hold these fast in head and heart
    nor dare depart their magic incantations.
Pulpit, prayer mat, whirling dance, turbans, cassocks,
    saffron robes, thunderous chords of organ pipes,
    soaring songs of joy and praise while millions die
    of bombs and blades and bloodied inquisitions
    —whose blistered lips and tortured tongues
    no longer sing or say them.
Come dance with me. A melody of gnostic notes.
A dance with mystic wings of hope
    unchained by facts defining.

Come dance with me. Deity, humanity,
    pared in joyful harmony.
No literal this, no literal that, no lists,

no plenary scripts of holy writ.
A mutual dance that celebrates
redeeming myths that birth a new awakening.
Waltzing with the least, the lost,
rising from our sacred pews,
wondering why the doors are closed,
and puzzled by our sayings.
No more hesitation. No more isolation.
Come dance with me
The words are yours, the rhythm yours,
The melody is LOVE.

Called, Claimed, Named

God, you have called, claimed, and named us.
From wooded grove to swirling spire
you've guided our faltering steps.
You've wept in our weakness and rejoiced in our strength.
You've swept aside shadows of doubt,
forgiven our reluctance to let go of lesser things,
and challenged us with new horizons.
Bless us to truly be a community that bears your son's name.
Open our hearts, minds, and will to its call.
May its circumference encircle all
who seek joy, hope, love, and peace.
May it define us and redefine us.
May it bless your wounded Earth
setting at liberty creatures great and small.
Free us from fear. Dispel our hesitancy. Help us rediscover our call
to be faithful witnesses of Christ's community
in daily word and deed. Amen.

Moses Moments

Step back. Take a breath. Listen carefully to the other voice
— the one you prefer not to hear. The one calling you to ministry.
"Surely, there are others, Lord. Call them. Send them."
Step back. Take a breath. Listen to the voice that says, "Slow down.
It's not settled." Listen to the voice that reminds you of your tendency to rush
to judgment—to declare the verdict is in signed, sealed, delivered.

Whenever you preference what you think you know, and what you
   think is right at the cost of what IS right, the case is always closed.
   "Surely, there are others, Lord. Call them. Send them. LOOK!
   ENOUGH! You have the wrong person. They'll never believe me.
   I'm not eloquent. Send someone else. Why isn't that bush burning?"
Life's little Moses' Moments. Step back. Take a breath. Listen carefully to the
voice: "Slow down. It isn't settled. Trust me—there is far more to you than
you think there is!"

Reflection: U-turns Permitted

More is lost than gained when we resist peeling back the layers of what we think we believe. Hesitant to be cast afloat on oceans of uncertainty, we rarely plumb the depths of theological discovery. It takes courage to plunge in, tread water, and gasp for air amid stormy seas hoping for a lifeline. I believe it is vital to dive in over and over again in search of fuller understandings of self, others, the cosmos and "God" or whatever deep reality calls to us

I constantly remind myself that my ideas of God are not God! I know what it is to be landlocked by past perceptions. I also realize my current slippery grip on life's mysteries shall inevitably slide away in favor of insights presently beyond my grasp. On the other hand, theological exploration is not a process of abandoning all previously held understandings in favor of the latest wispy wind of doctrine on the rise. Ideologies that jettison one's core ethical principles (love, kindness, integrity, compassion, forgiveness, the worthiness of each expression of life, etc.) are unworthy of allegiance. Faith's journey presents countless pathways. U-turns are permitted.

Where the Light Gets In

A little light breaks through our dimness, now and then, shining brightly
amid the gloom of dusty days and soaring sunlight's smiling face. Good days
and not so good, it will have its way this sprinkle of lightness that laugh
away the brooding soul, the angst of strained beliefs, the dance of questions
unresolved and teasing. Each soul has cracks within—for, as the poet muses,
"That's where the light gets in." Nor can it be contained in somber, shrouds
of silence spun by death's dark hand. Stardust has its way—springing forth in
little acts of kindness: a smiling face, a moment's grace, a sip of understand-
ing. A drop of goodness here and there: a wink, a nod, a word of care, a hurt
absorbed, forgiven and forgotten. One brief life unlettered by the masses,
asleep before Love's time, And yet, her spark remains unspent—her impact
softly glowing—a little splash of shining hope shimmering in the simplest act
that spells her name in what we say and do.

Wife, Mother, Teacher, Leader
Lyda McMurray

Lyda McMurray is an intelligent, creative, innovative, and extremely well organized, wife, mother, and teacher. It is a toss-up as to who has the edge in terms of talent between Lyda and husband, Brian. The phrase, *"They were meant for each other"* is cliché but it fits this couple who stand by, with, and for, each other. Highly respected by her peers, Lyda was awarded teacher of the year at Cordill Mason elementary school and is noted for her imaginatively decorated classrooms. She holds a master of informational science and learning technologies degree, but her priority and passion is her family.

Lyda loves to cook and dabbles in interior design. If one thing perpetually spills out of Lyda—it is "JOY!" She summarizes her response to life in these words, *"I'm always intrigued by learning new ways to be happy, show gratitude, and be the best person I can be."*

One word that describes both Lyda and Brian is "enthusiastic." Yes, they are attractive, have engaging personalities, and see the sunny side of life even when it's raining, but that is not why I describe them as enthusiastic. The derivation of the word "enthusiasm" is *entheos* meaning "divinely inspired, possessed by a god," (from *en* "in" + *theos* "god") In this sense, enthusiasm (the process of God being in you) is the highest compliment one can receive. Lyda and Brian share "enthusiasm" with everyone they meet.

BRIAN McMURRAY:

"To put it concisely, Lyda is an incredible woman whose presence makes me better every day. I know it's cliché, but I honestly am not sure what I'd do without her. From the day we met I've been in love with her. (She's incredibly easy to fall in love with.) I'm never been as comfortable, or happy, around another human being as I am with Lyda. She enhances my life in so many ways. We laugh often (she's one of the funniest people I've ever met), but we also challenge each other. Lyda is my favorite collaborator. Our brains work so well together. We enjoy doing creative projects together. Our energy feeds off the other. It's a wonderful partnership. Creative, smart, funny, compassionate, and beautiful—Lyda is the center of our family, and the love of my life."

ῆills to Climb

Off with the old, on with the new.
Diets launched, treadmills dusted off,
*   miles reset to "zero," and digital hills to climb.*
Thin clothes hanging on the line waiting, baiting, anticipating.
A new you crying to get out,
*   shedding years, tears, and cardiac fears.*
"I will be young and beautiful."
Resurrection! Just a push-up away.
A brand new year of gizmos, gadgets, and fashion consultants:
"Blue is in—red is out!" And what of green, God?
In or out? Out or in?
Birds, trees, mountains, and seas,
*   melting ice flows, polluted breeze.*
A million empty rice bowls in lands afar and near,
*   hope reset to "zero" stained with mother's tears,*
*   bullets, bombs, and brave young lads*
*   replaced by neatly folded flags.*
In or out? Out or in? So many hills to climb!

When the Stone is Rolled Away

I have a friend who thinks he's alive.
He isn't. He eats, sleeps, walks, talks, and races through the day.
A short day. Never long enough.
When he does die, it will be just a matter of lying down,
    closing eyes that are already closed.
He knows better, of course. He knows he's dead
    —because he'll tell you.
He occasionally tells himself,
    "I must slow down, I'll do better tomorrow."
He won't, of course. He can't. It's easier being dead than alive.
I meet a lot of dead people, God. They're just like me.
But every so often, resurrection comes,
    when everything stops
    and nothing starts except your heart again.
A lick of sunshine on the cheek, a breeze around my ears,
    a flash of feathers on the wing.
Grayness drains. Colors pop.
There are feet inside my shoes, and I know it.
There's honey on my tongue, and I taste it.
There's silence all around and I hear it.
There's a song I've never sung, and I sing it.
Brief little awakenings. A minute here and there
    when the stone is rolled away
    and I wonder why I ever stayed inside.

Details

Snap-shot. Glamour shot. Things said and done? The life and times of God's
own son penned in holy ink. Miracles, majesty, hillside talks and parables,
death and resurrection—soon to come again? Have you read your story,
Jesus? Do you recognize your name? Is this man a stranger? Have we made
you whom you're not? Are details unimportant? Fact? Fantasy? Is good
news spun in metaphors and every child begotten?

Presence

I walk the streets in ragged clothes. I'm on the bus beside you. I laugh and run in children's shoes. I'm old. I'm young. I'm stout. I'm thin. I'm everywhere that life begins and ends. My spirit lives within you.

God, help me see your hidden face in every soul I meet to today.
Help me be your living peace, your hands, your feet, your gentle
voice that speaks release to all who seek shalom.

I yearn to save the groaning Earth, the lost, the torn, the fractured souls who cry for worth. Salvation's more than sin's release. It finds the lost. It offers peace. It feeds the poor. It liberates. It opens hearts. It heals, redeems, and reconciles. It walks, talks, and lives shalom.

Cost What it May

"Seek for truth; come whence it may, lead where it will, cost what it may."
Cost WHAT it may? So easy to say, but can we?
Can we strip away truths we think are true?
Lessons taught. Beliefs caught. Miracles and iffy things:
  a God that's one, yet three, a savior hanging on a tree,
  an empty tomb, angel's wings, dead that walk
  ancient psalms and prophecies?

"What is truth?" Pilate's plea unanswered rings.
Give it space. Give it time. It's a matter of holding on and letting go
  —a willingness to take faith's leap
  —to trust that truth fears no examination,
  no self-fulfilling confirmation.
Truth is a journey where what was may be shaken by what is.
Where boundless revelation denies reiteration.
Where faith is free to sail seas of exploration
  —no turning back, no land-locked declarations.
Come sail with me: "Seek for truth; come whence it may,
  lead where it will, cost what it may."[48]

New Beginnings
Avery Adamson Peters

I remember iceboxes. I remember the iceman, iron tongs in hand, hefting huge blocks of ice—his vein-popping arms casually dismissing their weight. I remember fifteen-cent, grainy, black and white movie serials: Flash Gordon, Roy Rogers, Gene Autry, Lash La Rue—unblemished heroes saving damsels in distress Saturday after Saturday (everyone fully dressed and "dang it" the only expletive). I remember horse-drawn milk wagons. I remember radio shows: The Creaking Door, The Shadow, Lux Radio Theater, Henry Aldridge, Amos and Andy (try broadcasting it today), Fibber McGee and Molly. "Tune in next week"—and we did! I remember five-cent Cokes, summer vacations stretching for an eternity, lined note scribblers, snapping popsicles in half, cap-guns, towels for "capes," and thick corduroy knickers that should have been restricted to mounted police officers. I hated knickers. I remember when people talked face to face.

Today, I have an iPhone, iPad, Kindle, MacBook Pro computer, wireless speakers, a 3D flat screen TV, Amazon Echo (are you listening, Alexa?), and friends whose faces I never see—their thumbs texting messages while nodding occasionally during live conversations with a friend.

Look, it *is* "A Wonderful Life," Jimmy Stewart—an age of miracles and science fiction compared to ice tongs, milk bottles with U-shaped cream-filled tops, comic books, and radio shows! Today's kids have tablets, drones, and cellphones. Today, everyone is a photojournalist, a blogger, Facebook poster, Tweeter, or Instagramer. Ironically, digital communication overload may be driving us further and further apart.

I gaze at one-year-old Miss Avery Adamson Peters, and I have no inkling of what brave new world awaits her. Fact is, it doesn't wait for her; it doesn't wait for anyone. The good old days of "now" are seemingly only nanoseconds from becoming passé, "you've got to be kidding," days. Current data suggests all human knowledge is doubling every thirteen months. It's mind-boggling. I pray tomorrow will not bring a pill or implant device to replace my morning coffee or a personalized avatar that will drink it for me, tell me I enjoyed it, and leave me high and dry. Most of all, I pray Miss Avery will have someone to actually talk with.

New Wonders

Those eyes, those big blue eyes, and dimpled thighs,
*   her whispered sighs attempting words by sounds absurd.*
She's gazing here and gazing there and wondering if the smiles
*   and stares from everywhere will still be there and still will care*
*   when tomorrow births new wonders.*

A Moment for Living

A cup of coffee, a piece of pie, a friendly handshake, just you and I sharing a
sunset, a walk in the rain, a smile, a touch, a soft refrain, a hand-scrawled
note, a warm embrace, a breath of silence, a simple place, a holy place,
where wrinkles and warts and silly mistakes are covered by laughter, and
everyone takes a moment for living, loving and grace.

Silent Dreams

Let me lay down silent dreams that never sing their waking songs
*   nor see the break of dawn. Asleep within myopic hopes unuttered and*
undone, they whisper wails of "might have been,"
of virgin places still unseen, of books unread, of love unsaid,
and wondrous landscapes yet to tread. Let me lay down liturgies
and fantasies and supernatural gods. Let me birth a brand-new day
where creedal claims are cast away, where resurrection spells my name,
discerning all that comes my way, both holy and profane.

Let me lay down ageless hurts delivered and received,
   the festered thorns of painful deeds,
   a word, a glance, an unspent chance
   to heal Love's dance when friendships are not whole.
Let me lay down safety's chains that bind my tongue from speaking out
   when fairness, truth, and equality are strangled by inequity
   and saying all that should be said
   remains unsaid for fear of losing face.
Let me live each day by grace, defeating hesitation's place
   —the politics of self-deceit that justifies my sluggish feet
   from answering Love's clear call.
Let me stand on higher ground and sing my dreams awake.

No One Is Listening

Faces stretched on newsprint. Black. White. Splashes of color.
Blogged, beaten, bruised, or praised. Nameless, blameless,
   invisible people, their soundless cries straining to be heard
   above catchy tabloid headlines.
You and I holding them, folding them, throwing them away.
Here today, gone tomorrow.
A parade of pixilated personalities pressed between pages,
   Facebook posts "Liked" or disliked, digitally stealing the day.
Car bombs, candidates, winners, and losers.
Bold font villains and heroes—the litany goes on
   —good news, bad news, 'fake news,' no news.
Fifteen seconds of fame where forgotten names
   are lost, looped, taped and trapped, just a mouse click away.
Sound bites of presidents, despots, and kings,
   political pundits who tell it their way:
   who's to the right and who's to the left,
   who's in the lead and who's left behind,
   who can we trust and who's not a friend.
Infomercials, wide-screen TVs, Big Brother watching,
   hawking his wares, selling us things we suddenly need.
Tummy tucks, implants, facelifts, and dreams,
Time in a bottle—lotions and creams,
Waistbands and wrinkles the eye can't detect
   —special effects without the effect.
Fingers on keyboards seldom touching a friend,
   relationships locked on a monitor screen.
Somewhere a child is crying, and no one is listening.

Little Lessons

Tender years, wonder years where "Yes!" and "No!" are born:
   "No, no, must not touch." "No, no, honey, put that down."
   "Yes, yes, give it to Mummy." "Be gentle, be nice."
Life's little lessons for life's little people.
Innocence wed to curiosity—reaching out, touching, tasting,
   wondering, never waiting. A first step followed by another
   —a world of wonder as close as dimpled hands, bright eyes,
   listening ears, and a tasting tongue can explore.
Fire and ice. A sting. A tear. A crinkled face.
A cry. A smile. Squeals of delight.
A "ring-around-the-rosy time" of bumps, bruises,
   and Band-Aids, where tiny toes run on empty
   "until we all fall down."
Love them. Hold them. Protect them.
Teach them life's little lessons. Two little lessons!
That's all! As simple and profound as
   when to say yes and when to say no.
Joy, sorrow, life and death, the very cosmos rests on yes and no,
   the sorting of priorities in a world where back-worn ball caps
   mirror a world where much is turned around.
Life's little lessons for life's little people:
   when to say yes and when to say no.
YES! to honesty, respect, courtesy, generosity,
   responsibility, self-discipline.
YES! to sensitivity, sacrifice, compassion, and kindness.
YES! to earth, wind, fire, and rain
   —the splendor of this planet upon which we stand,
   the seas on which we sail, the stardust that we are.
"YES" to God's unmerited grace
   —the very breath of life's joy, hurts, healing, and hope.
"YES!" to the chance to begin again
   and a resounding "NO!" to everything and anything,
   large or small, that reduces who you are called to be
   lest we "ALL" fall down.

Reflection: To Nurture, Care, Protect, and Promise

When we baptize, consecrate or bless a child we are not in this act reminding God of the innocence, beauty and budding potential of a vision of life to be. We are not reminding God to bless and protect this fragile and infinitely important life. God needs no reminding. We need reminding! We need to be reminded that LOVE has given each young life to our trust and keeping—that each so-called "ordinary" child is to be loved not just equally, but uniquely. The birth of every child is God's YES to the world!

Each Life—God's "Yes!"

Each new born life we celebrate—God's treasure still unwrapped.
Contained within each child of hope are promises untapped.
Love BIRTHED. Loved CHOSEN. Held fast in parent's arms.
Teen, adult, middle-age, crowding senior years—your child remains your
*   child, protected from life's stormy days, from fears and war's alarms.*
Love defeats the calendar. Far, near, or gone before their time;
*   they never leave your arms.*
Each child's a living sacrament, enfolded in God's grace,
*   wrapped within family, friend, or a stranger's smiling face.*
Birthed within creation's soul, faith remains aglow.
For each new life's a miracle—God's "Yes" to every "No."

Peace-Maker, Forth Teller
Grant McMurray

"GRANTaMUSEd" is the name of Grant McMurray's Internet blog through which he shares insightful wit and wisdom wrapped in eloquence. He certainly qualifies as one who enriches the lives of countless people and causes for good. In Grant's case, good is an anemic qualifier. He has dedicated himself to the pursuit of peace throughout his ministerial career, his writings, love of history, firsthand appreciation of global cultures, and his daily life. Grant is anything but "ordinary." Where many writers struggle over sentence structure and clarity, Grant dashes off coherent thoughts with an economy of words jammed with artful clarity.

Grant served as prophet-president of the *Community of Christ* for eight years. His reframing of the office of prophet-president was a major gift to his denomination. He emphasized the church was not "a people with a prophet" but a community of "prophetic people." Grant helped church members understand prophesy is not spiritual fortune telling. The Hebrew prophets were not "foretellers" who mystically predicted predestined events but were "forth-tellers" who boldly spoke truth to power challenging political, religious and societal injustice in all its malignant forms contextual to their times. Grant maintained that mature faith calls for prophetic leadership together with a prophetic people committed to confront systemic injustice and inequity. Under his leadership, "We Proclaim Jesus Christ and Promote Communities of Joy, Hope, Love and Peace" became the church's mission statement and call to action.

Grant's leadership contributions are beyond the scope of this brief profile and best left to future historians. Nevertheless, the following score high on my list: his willingness to listen to the opinions of others; his passion to see the church become "a people dedicated to the pursuit of peace and healing of the Spirit"; his courage to set specific, measurable targets for growth and expansion under the banner "Transformation 2,000;" and his guidance to rename the church, "Community of Christ"—not as a denial of its rich heritage—but as a clarion call to redefine and understand its mission in the present age.

In retirement, Grant's innate ability to probe deeply into the marrow of contemporary issues (political, cultural, moral, controversial) and insightfully turn them on their ear for a fresh new hearing is remarkable. A wordsmith "forth-teller" whether as writer or spellbinding speaker, Grant combines insightful wisdom with belly busting humor and emotive intelligence:

"I tend to look at my life in segments, not to ignore the essential unity of the whole, but to see the pieces that compose it. Here are the segments:

"The Canadian Years (1947-1959)

I consider myself a Canadian even though I lived there only twelve years and am a naturalized US citizen. I visited frequently and have relatives and friends there. The real reason I know I am a Canadian, however, is that every time I read or hear the word my skin tingles and my ears prick up. That doesn't happen with Mozambique.

"The Growing up American Years (1959-1965)

These are basically my secondary education years, in which I learned that a chesterfield was a cigarette and not a couch and had to explain that hockey was not played on a horse. (I also learned that my treasured hockey card of Maurice "Rocket" Richard wasn't worth a damn.)

"The College/Seminary What I Want to be
When I Grow Up Years (1965-1971)

I knew that when I graduated from William Chrisman High School in 1965, I would go to Graceland College. How did I know? Because my family told me so. I planned for go two years and then transfer to the University of Missouri School of Journalism. Instead, I ended up getting mixed up with my patriarchal blessing, missionaries, reunions, and such. I ended up staying at Graceland majoring in religion and English, and then enrolling in the master of divinity degree at St. Paul School of Theology. It made no sense whatsoever, but I guess it worked out okay.

"The Community of Christ Years—Dealing with the Past (1971-1982)

I served the church for 33 years, and that falls rather neatly into three components, none of which I was qualified for. While finishing seminary, I needed work and the church hired me for a stint in the history department, and then as Church Archivist (a job first held by Noah), and then as Director of Library-Archives Services, and later as Assistant History Commissioner. That was ten years; and I consider these as my time dealing with the past.

"The Community of Christ Years—Dealing with the Present (1982-1992)

In 1982, the First Presidency asked me to take on the role of World Church Secretary. This is something like the chief bureaucrat of the church, managing minutes and records and serving as Executive Assistant to the First Presidency. I considered it the best job in the church. You were at the center of everything that was going on, knew the ways decisions were made, but didn't have to take responsibility for any of it. It had never been seen as a pathway to top leadership positions, but in many respects, it was excellent experience. This was also ten years in the making and I considered it a time where I had to work with the administrative components of the church—dealing with the present.

"The Community of Christ Years—Dealing with the Future (1992-2004)

When President Smith called me to serve as his Counselor in the First Presidency, and four years later as his successor as President of the Church, I knew that my work with past and present would now be handled by others. From this time forth my focus must be on discerning where God calls us as a prophetic people beyond the horizon and into the future.

"The Retirement Years (2004 - TBA)

Parkinson's Disease. Do I hear an AMEN?

"The Summing Up:

My Personal Mission Statement: In family and society, I will work to build community by embracing heritage, valuing diversity, and pursuing peace."

Prophets' Song

The words they speak are not their own—a song beyond their keeping. Formed from lips and lifted tongue it soars and sails on wings of hope like fragile thoughts of wounded truth whose webs of light stretch heart and soul to heights of understanding. Pleading. Partial. Incomplete. Words forever wanting. Each prophet-poet dreams and weeps. They seek to sing the Spirit's song so we may hear its pleadings, yet know that all they strive to say, captures but a fleeting note for those within its hearing. Canonized. Digitized. Inky words on onionskin. Love's porous alphabet of grace received yet ever leaking.

Truth's Unmasking

Wisdom couched in holy writ stirred by truth's unmasking, re-frames the deeds of heart and soul intent on life's full living. It reaps applause from those who see, yet dulls the sight of clouded eyes, whose scales defuse light's bidding. Ink-trapped words remain stillborn made mute by mindless reading. They cannot breathe. They have no hands, no feet, no flesh, no blood, no incarnation waiting, when listening ears lack wings to soar beyond their printed meaning.

Christ Bids Our Hearts to Sail[49]

The hidden seas within the soul, Christ bids our hearts to sail,
    to face the winds and waves of change with courage to prevail.
To cast away from safety's shore, unfettered by our fear,
    and float on faith above the storm assured that Christ is near.
To deeper depths, Christ beckons us, our calling to discern,
    with winds of hope to stir our quest to understand and learn.
Content no more in shallow streams our purpose to explore,
    the truth of who we're called to be, down deep within faith's core.
The name of Christ defines our call—it shapes our destiny
    to share the vision of God's peace as Christ's community
    whose common task—with cultures vast—creation can redeem.
We hold life's keys to plot the course to realize God's dream.

Spaces in Between

We speak a river of sound—words without letters, spaces, separation— pausing only for a breath here and there to sustain our wanting song. No spaces in between. Just sound. Words seamlessly jumbled together in a melody of meaning captured by ear and spliced by the mind. Spaces in between give meaning to the score. Each note, separate from the other— lifting, falling, holding, hardening, softening, sweeping to conclusion— beginning where they end. Birth. Death. Something in between. MORTALITY. This glorious NOW! This sacred space freed from everlasting. And they who postpone heaven are not alive at all.

Deeper Self[50]

Show us, God, our deeper self: sister earth,
  sister sky, soil and soul united, each drop of rain,
  each bird's refrain—the very air we breathe—we ARE!
Wind, wave, wounded landscapes, creatures great and small,
  groan for liberation yet we hear them not at all.
Each muffled sigh, each muted cry—a voice that is our own,
  —our deeper self, our "otherness," not nature's prayer alone.
The music of creation plays not for us,
  for we are but a single note added to its song
  whose cosmic composition flows for eons lost and long.
Our one brief note, so late upon the scene,
  self-glorified, self-amplified, yet barely heard or seen.
Let it harmonize, not patronize,
Let it bless, not burden. Heal, not hurt.
Let it join with all that is God's rhapsody of peace.
We are one. We are many.
We are the Earth—walking, talking, breathing
  —praying for release.

Delicate Balance[51]

Days continue to fold in on each other. Not a blurring of time, just its natural flow. Natural flow? My, how that phrase slips off my tongue so cavalierly. I must not escape the wonder of it all. This fortuitous concourse of atoms that makes up me and all the other MEs, blackholes, asteroids, comets, planets, and things unnamed swimming and spinning in space, light years apart and as close as next door. And here I sit on this blue orb that rotates at just the right angle, the precise orbit, not too close and not too far from a fiery star— that grants me warmth and life. This tiny round spec whirling for eons on gravity's string, a hair's degree from fire and ice. A delicate balance. A mixture of stardust and hope. A remarkable blending of gasses, wind, water, soil and sea bubbling up the soup of life. And perhaps, most astonishing of all, "consciousness"—to be awake and aware of this splendid mystery. And more than that—much more—to think that I may address the One who puts it all in play. Quirks, and quarks, and deity. Such a delicate balance—to reach out, teetering at the edge of thought itself, to touch the finger of God and sense a smiling face.

Reflection: Woven Together

Life is relationships. We have barely crossed the threshold of a postmodern world view where quantum physics is redefining perceptions of reality. The word "universe" is reclaiming its root meaning, i.e., "one-reality" in that all that was, is and will be is inexplicably connected and one. No sharp line separates the sacred and the secular. As the Qumran texts remind us, we are the product of a very special union, "a sacred marriage between the soul of the heavens and the tissue of the world."[52]

We relate to the past, the present, the anticipated future, others, self, God, and a myriad of complex relationships wrapped up in the very cosmos itself. We are not only shaped by these relationships—we shape them for good or ill. The gospel calls for the right or righteous arrangement of relationships. We are challenged to restore healthy relationships, which is at the heart of faith's journey.

We are called to respond to the plight of those trapped by circumstance, limited choice, and the cries of the earth for deliverance and new birth. Life is not a solo act; its tapestry is multifaceted. It is woven together with diverse threads, all of which are God's chosen fabric!

Trailings

To search no more the ink of night with sleepless eyes.
To gaze no more an autumn's blaze.
To no more savor sweet or sour,
    or hear the sounds of surf and shore,
    a newborn's cry, a lover's sigh,
    the silence of a snowflake's fall.
To see no more the eyes of one whom I adore
    who fills a void I cannot fill.
Pages torn from life's brief score
    are swallowed far too soon.
Yet countless songs and memories shall not pass away.
The heartbeat of a life lived well shall not be silent stilled.
Love's rhythm stirs trailings of the soul
    —agonies, victories, calm amid the storm,
    the sharing of a word, a deed, a kindly act, a card, a note,
    a touch of hope when midnight comes at noon.
A listening ear, laughter's balm, lessons earned and learned.
Yes, the sun will set when evening's nigh
    but these shall never die.

"never Second-Besc"
Joyce Lorance McMurray

Grant McMurray quickly would admit his marriage to Joyce Lorance McMurray is the best thing that ever happened to him. Joyce is not one who seeks the limelight. She shies away from what she interprets as undue notice of her skills and achievements.

Joyce worked in the Fort Osage School District from 1977 until retirement in 2012. She taught third and fifth grade and in 1993 began working as a middle school library specialist having earned a master's degree in library science and information services. She consistently re-invented her school library with innovative and creative displays that transformed it into an incredible place for students and teachers alike.

Teaching and exposing young people to new worlds of learning was a calling, not a career. She describes her work in the following words.

"I love the challenge of matching young adults to books. One of my greatest pleasures is bringing award-winning authors to Fire Prairie

125

Middle School each year and collaborating with classroom teachers to plan challenging research opportunities for kids. In addition, I coordinate our school annual Family Literacy Night event to bring kids, staff, families and authors together. I love the variety of creative challenges provided in my job."

Joyce never settles for second-best. In brief, Joyce does ordinary things in an extraordinary way, bringing creativity, energy, and excellence to every endeavor. She knits, cooks, mothers, and keeps Grant in check (or at least tries to). Her proudest role to date is "grandmother" to two adorable grand-daughters. Her imprint on their lives will be indelible. DNA is wonderful, but it never replaces a listening ear, a loving touch, and a warm heart.

Here and Now

Heaven sings in every subtle summer breeze,
*   in crashing waves on sandy shores,*
*   in silence sliced by feathered starling's song.*
Heaven sings and shouts creation's holy name
*   in wonders that escape our muted ears and hurried sight.*
Robbed of that which spells God's name
*   we yearn to knock on heaven's door*
*   and strain to find its sacred-shore*
*   beyond the pale of all that is.*
Fumbling, stumbling, unaware—
*   we fail to see that heaven's home*
*   is here—is now, IS everywhere.*

There Should Have Been a Jesus

Bruised, broken, blotches of blue. Split lip. Swollen cheek.
She's somebody's mother, somebody's wife,
*   somebody's damaged goods.*
There should have been a Jesus! Someone who saves.
*   Someone who steps in when the whole world steps out.*

Young, strong, bright, clean, caring, considerate, and kind.
A good Christian boy silently gay. Hiding himself.
Afraid to come out, living a lie despite of himself.
Smiling yet crying and shouting inside.
Somebody's brother, somebody's son, somebody's damaged goods.
There should have been a Jesus! Someone who saves.
*   Someone who steps in when the whole world steps out.*

His lips too thick, his nose too broad, his skin too dark
  to make the grade. Living thin acceptance.
Pushing at a ceiling always out of reach.
Somebody different? Somebody less? Somebody's damaged goods?
There should have been a Jesus! Someone who saves.
  Someone who steps in when the whole world steps out.

Incense, prayer mats, and pentagrams. Kosher food and whirling dance,
  holy fires and holy texts. Gods, goddesses and sacred chants.
Somebody's way, somebody's praise, somebody's faith
  supposedly not quite as pure, not quite as true?
There should have been a Jesus! Someone who saves.
Someone who steps in when the whole world steps out.
Collateral damage. Friendly fire. Car bombs, missiles,
  preemptive attacks. Ethnic cleansing and empty bowls.
Children with AIDS wearing no clothes.
There should have been a Jesus! Someone who saves.
  Someone who steps in when the whole world steps out.
Despised, rejected, nailed to a tree. Stripped, beaten,
  wounded, and whipped. Begotten, forgotten, exposed, and betrayed.
Somebody's hope, somebody's rage,
  somebody's servant, somebody's son.
There should have been a Jesus! Someone who saves.
Someone who steps in when the whole world steps out.
  Someone like you and me.

Stirrings

*This strange stirring within, never fully absent, softly sifting through the
milieu of what is and what is not. The fabric of who I think I am unraveled by
constant rending of the mind. Questions that refuse to sleep. The mysteries of
faith spun from cultural threads. Stories told of angel wings, of crosses
raised, and empty tombs. "Iffy" things and miracles, epic tale, and parables.
The building of a life by songs of faith and wonder. Yes, wonder. This hope
that has a handle. I carry it. It carries me. But where and why? And what if
all were swept away? The breeze of rationality that says it cannot be. Down
deep within my revelry the folds of faith unfurl my soul—a birth that's ever-
blooming. Its petals seek a warmer light freed from obligation—stripped
clean of dogma's deathly dance and lists of wounded sayings. Its itch cannot
be served nor scratched by certitude and blessings. Sweet queries, doubts,
and fantasies. A thirst that's never quenched —an open door, a hill to climb
each morn a new arising. It will not let me go.*

Face to Face[53]

When I can ache with hunger pangs
 for those whose bowls are washed with tears
 and thirst to quench the driest tongue
 and visit those who live in fear
 and hold the hands of captive souls
 who sit alone when death is near,
I see in them Christ's face divine
 and hope they see his face in mine.

When I can fill a stranger's need
 with friendship's hand and plant hope's seed
 that bears love's fruit and brings relief
 to heavy hearts weighed down with grief
 and share Christ's peace that brings release
 from burdens born by hurt's increase
I see in them Christ's face divine
 and hope they see his face in mine.

When I can share another's pain
 and bring to birth life's joy again
 with loving deeds that break each chain
 that binds a wounded heart's refrain.
When I esteem each soul on earth
 as blessed by God with priceless worth
I see within Christ's face divine
 and hope his face is seen in mine.

When I can hear God's many names
 in whirling dance and candle flames,
 in incense prayed and prayer mats laid,
 in songs and psalms and Wailing Wall.
When I can hear in one and all
 of every sacred book God's call
I'll see in life Love's face divine
 and hope it sees Love's face in mine.

Everyone Counts
Stan Mengel

"After-Thought" was my initial heading for Stan Mengel but realized many would miss the hyphen and think I included Stan as an *afterthought*. It was a not-so-clever attempt to emphasize that Stan, a retired economics educator, is someone who carefully thinks before he acts! When I hear the word, economist, I envision a bespectacled number cruncher enraptured by pie charts and mind-boggling statistics intent on deciphering the mysteries of gas pump prices, stock market agitations, and why my budget decries, *"There is too much week at the end of the money!"[54]

Stan graduated from the University of Missouri-Columbia with general honors as well as department honors in both economics and political science. He received his graduate education in economics at Stanford University, where he was a Woodrow Wilson and a Stanford-Wilson fellow. He taught at several universities including the University of Santa Clara, Ohio University, Akron University, and Lesley University in Cambridge, Massachusetts.

Stan held the Firestone Chair at Akron University and was Pietz professor of economic education at Lesley University where he was director of the
National Center of Economic Education for Children. Stan retired in 2008
from the Economics Department at the University of Missouri-Kansas City,
where he was president of the Missouri Council on Economic Education. He
was instrumental in creating the Truman Medal for Economic Policy awarded
biennially to a leading national economist by the Truman Library. Stan also
created a one-semester course in personal finance and economics, now
taken by 65,000 students each year as a Missouri high-school graduation
requirement.

Stan is far more than his educational and career achievements. This
economist is not a "bean counter"; he is a "people counter"! Stan is committed to broadening public understanding of the ways that economic forces
shape individuals and societies, believing that greater understanding will
bring improved decision-making and well-being.

For Stan "everyone counts, or nobody counts," (a phrase borrowed from
author Michael Connelly's Detective Harry Bosch novels). This motto defines
who Bosch is, what he does, and why he does it. It is a moral principle
everyone should follow, and it accurately describes Stan. He serves as a
self-sustaining ordained minister with his wife, Gail, and contributes his
unique skills and pastoral ministry within and beyond the walls of Walnut
Gardens Community of Christ's sanctuary!

Reflection: Flat Screen Living

Flat screen friends old, young, smooth, wrinkled, handsome, plain, hero,
villain, victim—all of them yours, all of them you! The vicarious grin, the
laugh, the cool blue eyes. The mouth spewing anger's smoke and tears. A
million scenes of love, lament, and laughter. *All of it theirs. All of it yours.*
Life's scanty hopes and desperate dreams dancing on screens, teetering on
tongues like anemic incantations packaged for waiting ears eager to hear
your lines. Follow the script. Pursue the plot. Grip the viewer scene by scene.
Digital snacks of this and that to soothe the soul and starve the mind with
frozen thoughts stagnant and undone.

Who is this staring back from your 4K screen, with myriad memories
snuffed away, your waning years flown swiftly away and unrelenting? Time
gobbled. Unnourished by what could have been beyond this room: the kiss of
a summer's breeze, an autumn's blaze, a newborn's cry, a beat of wings,
peach juice coursing cheek and chin, a pinch of salt and pepper.

So, little gained. So, much lost. Books unread, landscapes unvisited, the
sting of salty tears, a paper cut, laughter's ring, fleeting brief awakenings. *All
of it theirs. All of it yours.* A trough of shallow appetites dulled by everydayness, and there you sit while others taste the day. Countless names and
faces. Products pitched and pandered. You live, die, and live again in
resurrection's easy chair transfixed by borrowed fantasies.

Are these voices theirs or yours? They must be! For you have auctioned
far too much to monitors and keyboards. Insular. Contained. Maintained. Life
lived at room temperature. No sweat. No pain. Each villain slain. So, near.

So, far! A cosmos at your fingertips: fast-forwarding what might have been.

Alas, you have saved the world a thousand times, defeated evil, soared through space, kissed the stars, and solved a million mysteries. You've fallen in love endless times with beauties half your age, climbed the highest mountain, sailed on countless seas, and NEVER touched a soul.

Step by Step

In every breath of spring, a new life is begun. In every drop of rain, there shines a thousand suns. In every starless night, there's promise of the dawn. In sunshine and in storm, hope still sings it song. In promises you make, In every step you take. You never walk alone; the Spirit's song plays on.

To Canonize

It isn't what you say—it's that you say it, God! We hear, rejoice, and revel in the security you're still there and speak to us, while millions burn candles, bathe, pray, spin, swirl, dance the dance, meditate, cogitate, scratch at heaven's door with songs and psalms, and much, much more. With hoping hands, we stretch and strain to touch eternity and fail to grasp the grace of now. Life's sacredness lies wrapped in everydayness, masked by dreams of pearly gates, golden streets and feathered angel wings. Speak to us, God. Say what you will. It matters not. Your voice alone shall satisfy. Rush. Rush. Raise hands and vote. Place holy letters in the Book. Sealed, revealed, concealed, congealed. The meal is served, and every plate is bare. It isn't what you say—it's simply that you say it, and we know that you're still there.

Inseparable[55]

Speak to us of your peace, Jesus. Not our peace: tight, limiting
— circumscribed by human wants and needs,
*   while creation groans, and we hear it not.*
We have placed ourselves far higher than we are.
From dust we come to dust we return.
We ARE the Earth betraying itself— euthanizing its wonder,
*   choking its air, stripping its streams, insatiably obliterating*
*   sister creatures great and small*
*   — hell-bent to dance our dance and have it all.*
Speak to us of a peace that doesn't sleep
*   — a peace that multiplies joys and divides sorrows,*
*   a peace that celebrates creation, a peace at war with separation,*
*   for to love one is to love all, and to wound one is to wound all.*

Reflection: Dropping Thees and Thous

Whose prayer is this? Mine, ours, yours? Can we set aside religious rhetoric? Drop our thees, thous, thine, praise, pleas, and petitions? Can we pause for a fleeting moment of silence stripped of our alphabet of grace, our holy unctions thinly disguised as favors sought and victories won? Can we candidly confess the mystery of prayer utterly confounds us? What did the psalmist sing? *"Before they call I will answer; while they are still speaking I will hear."* Does the omnipotence in which we've wrapped you render our hopes, thoughts, feelings, and stumbling words redundant before we speak them?

Does it matter? Are you "there," or are you "here," God? Are we praying to you, or are we praying to ourselves? Both. Because you are in us, and we are in you! We weave our wanting words and speak them *because to not speak them is to not live them!*

The blessing we pursue is simply this. We want to do what is right—not perfumed by hymns, homilies, and scriptural text, but fueled by integrity wed to compassionate service!

We want to be a blessing—one of healing, one of faith, of community wed to peace, forgiveness, justice, acceptance, and determination. One of choice and wise choosing! One of hope.

Hope leans forward, never sleepy or lazy, never fully defeated. Disappointed? Sometimes. Impatient? To be sure, but never throwing in the towel. May we lean forward, God celebrating what was, is, and will be: our wounds healed by your grace, our victories fueled by your love—our hope leaning far enough, long enough, patient enough to breathe-in your peace.

Reflection: Tight Fit

Squeezing God between the covers of a book is a very tight fit. Literalists are literalists selectively. Mining the Bible for inspiration, wisdom and enduring principles requires exploration—an exegetical exercise in "rightly dividing the word of truth." Sweeping scripture aside and devaluing its import because it houses contradictions and difficult passages is no less prejudicial than blindly accepting them as unsalable truths. Whenever we distill faith into definitive lists of dos and don'ts—whenever our tired definitions domesticate the mystery of the divine—wonder no longer claims us; we claim it and cut it down to size. The power of metaphorical language is its ability to couch within it more than facts or creedal declarations but something of the ethereal, that which escapes the discursive language of literalism. The bottom line is: Scripture is a vital guide, but it is not the inerrant "Word of God." God doesn't publish books.

All Are Welcome
Gail Mengel

In our weaker moments, we arbitrarily place people in circles of inclusion or exclusion (friends, enemies, rich, poor, the intelligentsia, the lost, the least, the labeled, etc.). Gail Mengel has dedicated herself to broadening the circle of inclusion for women's equality and religious ecumenism. She served on the Bi-National Advisory Council of the Center for the Prevention of Sexual and Domestic Violence (now known as the Faith Trust Institute) for more than twenty years. Gail directed an International Conference of Women (one of the dedicatory events for the Community of Christ Temple in Independence Missouri) that attracted 4,700 participants from more than twenty-eight nations.

The wonderful tag line of the United Methodist Church, "Open doors, open minds, open hearts" well describes Gail's passion for equity and inclusion. As with her husband, Stan, the motto, "Everyone counts, or nobody counts" also fits Gail's passion for equity and justice. She is a progressive thinker and doer committed to the principles of Shalom which embrace everything that makes for creation's highest good.

She served as a minister for Community of Christ for twenty years in a variety of leadership roles including director of women's ministries and as a World Church general officer who traveled extensively in many regions of the world. She was appointed as Community of Christ's first Ecumenical and Interfaith officer, representing it in more than twenty interfaith organizations, and was instrumental in her denomination acquiring membership in the National Council of Christian Churches. She was a Community of Christ representative to Church Women United and served as its eighteenth national president, 2004, 2008.

Gail has been active in community, school, and civic organizations, including leadership in the Parent Teacher Association, Scouting, League of Women Voters, and many nonprofit service organizations. She is a contributor and participant in Dining for Women (a program to help women and children in developing nations). She was elected to three four-year terms on the Board of Education in the Copley-Fairlawn School District in Ohio and served in leadership roles for the Ohio School Boards Association.

Her influence and ministry extend beyond her achievements. Gail continues to erase circles of exclusion that inhibit or prevent others from realizing their full potential. Her circle of "acceptance and worth of all people" has no circumference—everyone is welcome!

My Personal Credo[56]

Several years ago, I composed the following "personal mission statement." It was and continues to be challenging to live out. It reminds me that life is not all about me; it's about the right arrangement of relationships.

Live humbly. Live abundantly.
Start each day freed from the encumbrances of yesterday
    and filled with the gift of possibility.
Make the decision to be free. Live honestly, openly, and reverently.
Seek to put "first things first"
    and act with integrity in the moment of choice.
Ask with intent, listen without excuse, and act with courage.
Plan for the future but live in the present.
Be fully present to those you love,
    honoring their sacred independence,
    cherishing their love and respecting their mutuality.
Divide their sorrows and multiply their joys.
Consciously live in grace and share grace with others.
Bear positive witness of your faith while respecting the faith of others.
Distinguish between values and principles
    and put people before programs.
Be kind. Be gentle. Be patient.
Magnify your gifts and seek joyfully
    to make a positive difference within your circle of influence.
Live with enthusiasm, love with compassion,
    learn with humility, leave a legacy of hope.

Sleepers in the Street

Bread-baker, home-maker, parent, daughter, son.
Ticket-taker, laborer, children on the run.
The lost, the lonely, the weak, the strong,
  Million-dollar mansions—sleepers in the street.
Humanity, insanity, profanity—the list goes on and on.
Life wrapped in cold complexity
  redeemed by love's reality, here and now,
    not there and then.
A word. A touch. A song. A prayer. A smile. A note of care.
A hurt that's healed. A friend who's there.
A helping hand. A listening ear. The joy that laughter brings.
Salvation's song plays all day long in sunlight or in gloom.
Yet some who wait for pearly gates,
  for golden streets, and feathered wings,
    despite the brightest noon, stumble in the dark of day
    and cannot find their way.
Like sleepers in the street they yawn
  and dream the dream away.

Ah, So Good!

"And God saw that it was good!" Compared to what? Was this a second or
third try? Had there been practice runs? A string of slightly flawed creations,
marked-down and hung on a rack for early-bird shoppers? What makes for
good and not-so-good? Why is one face handsome and another not? Tall,
short, fat, and thin. Humanity's variety pack, cultured, measured, valued and
devalued. Wrong color, wrong vocabulary, wrong religion. Pews are in;
prayer mats are out? We journey through life searching for what's good.
Comparison, yes—competition, no! I need to shoot for the stars, God,
without putting myself in the basement. I need to stop worrying if I measure
up. No analysis, no dissections, no second thoughts, no "ah-shucks,
humility!" I need to say, "WOW! That was good!'—and rejoice in it.

Gentle Giant
Terry Read

On the bright sunny morning of November 17, 2015, midnight came at noon. Terry Read and his beloved Chihuahua, Kevin, fell victim to a fatal automobile accident. Midnight came to his loving wife, Linda. It came to his daughter, Andrea, and it came to everyone acquainted with this six-foot, seven-inch gentle giant whose quiet, unassuming, humanitarian life and ministry blessed friend and stranger alike.

Terry was a gifted competitive athlete, an award-winning writer, director, and producer of distance educational television with RXL Pulitzer before his ministerial career, but it was his extraordinary selfless response to the needs of others that set him apart as described in this excerpt from his obituary:

"His reach as a minister covered more than 100 congregations and touched thousands of people. Terry was a gentle and caring leader, a loving mentor and friend. He lived his concern for others daily, as he lived his commitment to social justice and inclusion. Terry led and served on many boards and committees, including Community of Christ's Human Rights Committee and various interfaith boards. Terry fought for a world in which every person would feel included and

cared for. He remained loyal through good times and bad, exactly the way he lived his life with all who knew him. A life lived in the service of others and God, is the life Terry chose from an early age. He was raised in the Community of Christ church, where he learned about what he called "being loved fiercely."

I never had a conversation with Terry that didn't include raucous laughter. He didn't simply sip life; he drank deeply. He loved life, and life loved him. Terry knew living and dying are rhythmic constants. We surrender to sleep's nightly burial to be awakened each day to resurrection. Resurrection shows its face in the rebirth of spring, victory over sickness, freedom from addiction, opportunity to "being again," repentance and forgiveness, broken relationships mended, or a life finding new meaning. Each day we die a thousand deaths. Death and resurrection happen minute by minute, second by second. In his unique and modest way, Terry sought to bring newness of life to everyone he met.

Terry's greatest joy was freeing people from injustice, racism, and all demeaning forms of labeling that consigned people to the death sentence of inequity. His ministry was not focused on life after death, but on life after birth —resurrection in the here and now. Terry knew the greatest threat to joy and fulfillment was not physical death but spiritual death: the death of kindness, the death of feeling and sensing others' needs, the death of laughing when others laugh and crying when others cry. Conversely, he understood abundant living required putting to death negative characteristics that diminish life: arrogance, greed, violence, prejudice, and self-centeredness! This is what made his death so tragic! His passing was magnified immeasurably because he died before all his dying was done!

When midnight comes at noon, when a loved one's life is senselessly cut down without rhyme or reason, desperation cries, "It was his appointed time!" "God called him home!" No, despite the good intentions of such sentiments, God did not call Terry home. Terry's *home* was California. Terry's *home* was his loving wife, beautiful daughter, his friends, colleagues, and the countless persons who drowned in his smile, laughed with his laughter, were touched by his helping hand, humility, ministry and abiding friendship. The God I worship had nothing to do with Terry's death. God does not circle dates on fate's calendar, nor does God call people home, because God's home is here as well as there.

What do you do when midnight comes at noon; when you mourn the passing of one who has died before all his dying was done? You lean forward assured that grace abides and will not let you go. You lean forward embracing love's other word: hope! Stained by tears, buoyed by laughter's memory, hope leans forward promising that joy, love, and peace will dance among our ashes. Believer, agnostic, or atheist, most of us yearn in our own way to be Easter-people—a people of new life and renewal—a people who not only claim hope but are claimed by it. Terry would remind friend and stranger alike that his God of hope sustains us through sunshine and shadow. Terry would want us to focus on the present, not the past. He would want us to work toward a desired future: a time, place, and condition where love is the heartbeat of relationships and community.

In This Very Room

In this very room are friends becoming family.
Thoughts, feelings, hopes, healings, questions, and concerns
    — all the stuff of life tucked within each person in this very room.
Some hidden, some not, some waiting beyond the margins
    where songs are song, prayers are prayed,
    wine is poured, and bread is shared.
In this room are a thousand stories, a thousand hopes and hurts,
    a thousand names who came before us, nurtured us and brought us here.
A thousand faces met and yet to meet, beyond this very room.
Common folk with uncommon dreams pinned to "iffy" beliefs
    and dim half-miracles that bind us together.
Here in this room, holy things happen
    caught between sweep second hands of worship,
    where for a fleeting moment we lay it on the line and say,
"Here, we are, Lord, not quite who we should be,
    but yours, nevertheless.
You are in us and we are in you ready to meet you
    in top hats, turbans, yarmulkes, hijabs, ball caps and fedoras
    beyond this very room
Be gentle. Be, gracious, God. We're here, sipping wine, breaking bread,
    waiting, wondering, hoping beyond hope
    in this very room. Amen.

Ink on a Page[57]

Ink on a page. Holy ink. Holy pages. Holy books. Hard-cover gods filled with insight, wisdom, and wonder. Proof-text permissions (Christian and non-Christian) that deny and destroy. It's all there in several versions—birth, death, demons, and deity—onionskin thin, fueling faith and fancy. It's a tight fit, God. We've squeezed you into chapters and verses. We've made you in our own image, put words in your mouth and used them for love and war. Open our eyes, ears, minds, and hearts to the rhythm of your Spirit that bares your love beyond words on a page. Free us from lethal literalism. Let sacred texts point the way, not "be" the way. Let them serve, not "be" served. Let them unite not divide. Let them, be a lamp unto our feet not a hammer in our hands.

What Matters Most
Steve and Cathi Veazey

The phrase "catch and release" comes to mind when I think of Steve and Cathi Veazey. Steve is an avid angler. Though fishing is usually not considered a spiritual practice, I suspect Steve would suggest otherwise. Amid sun-soaked sky and bubbling stream, Steve can be caught up in nature's beauty and released from life's competing voices that mute creation's wonder. Cathi, a gifted artist, captures beauty on canvas and through her camera lens. Both pastimes embrace a sense of "catch and release"—an opportunity to catch a glimpse of life's deeper reality released from everydayness. Catching fish and creating colorful renderings and photos, though important, are for Cathi and Steve secondary.

What matters most is experiencing the ordinary as extraordinary. Kate Chiles Graham in *Reaching the Thin Place* describes such moments of personal/spiritual awakening in these words, "The Eternal breaks in on the temporal and the temporal is prepared to receive it."[58] Obviously, there is far more to Cathi and Steve than rod, reel, brush, and camera. Ultimately, what matters most is their love for each other, their family, the worth of all persons, and their joint commitment to Christ.

An Ordinary Guy in a Not-so-ordinary Job

Steve has served Community of Christ as an apostle, director of Field Ministries, president of seventy, elder, church planter, youth leader, young adult minister, pastor, and the list goes on—a list that encompasses his life from toddler to teen, from teen to adult. A native of Paris, Tennessee, Steve has a bachelor of science in biology from the University of Tennessee, and a master of arts in religion from Park College, Parkville, Missouri. I am sure he would agree that a degree in religion and years of ministerial service did not fully prepare him for primary leadership of his denomination. How does one prepare for the demands of presidency and the call of prophetic guidance? The key to every role of ministerial service (member, deacon, priest, elder, etc.) is a willingness to exercise faith, give it your best, and trust God's grace.

Steve was ordained prophet-president of Community of Christ in 2005. His presidency has been sharply focused on discerning and clarifying Christ's mission for today's generation. The phrases "Christ's Mission, Our Mission" and "The Peace of Jesus Christ" are not mere tag lines; they are the overarching articles of faith energizing his life and ministry. He continues to promote these as "enduring principles and initiatives" that invite people to Christ, abolish poverty and suffering, pursue peace, develop disciples, and experience congregations in mission.

Putting First Things First and "Being There"

The foregoing easily describes an ordinary person leading an extraordinary life, but Steve is not defined by his ministerial gifts and responsibilities. Though he has immersed himself in the church, his ministry has not eclipsed his personhood. Cathi says:

"It would have been easy to make the church his primary focus, but he did not. When Steve became a husband and father in 1986, there was no doubt that family came first. There was never a time when his family questioned that loyalty and dedication. Steve put his own needs aside repeatedly for his family and his ministry. Steve is a kind and thoughtful man who is a reflective thinker. He spends great effort to study issues from many perspectives. That focus is reflected in all that he does. Steve's love of nature, especially water, is evident in his passion for fly fishing. Many times, he has said that he finds true peace when out on the water, casting a line. Sometimes, he relates catching a fish comes second to just being there."

Cathleen (Cathi) Diane (Henson) Cackler-Veazey

Cathi Cackler-Veazey, PhD, a native of Independence, Missouri, is a devoted disciple of Jesus Christ and ordained minister whose unique gifts of ministry are singularly compelling. Cathi serves as co-chair of the World Church Diversity Team and chair of Peace Pathways, a Community Christ affiliate that oversees the Children Peace Pavilion. She is involved in community volunteer work and management, serving on the Community Services

League (CSL) board and chair of the Independence Housing Authority by appointment of the mayor.

The word ordinary drops off the page when one considers Cathi's interests and labors. She has a background in strategic planning, leadership development, diversity education/advocacy, non-profit board leadership, career-transition consulting, human resources, and a personal passion for family research. Regrettably Cathi's full time church career of thirteen years ended to avoid any perception of conflict of interest when Steve was ordained president. Since then, Cathi and Steve have enjoyed numerous opportunities to travel and share in team ministry throughout the worldwide church, which has been a blessing.

Cathi is a lifelong learner. She attended Graceland University and received a bachelor of science in recreation/outdoor education from Indiana University. She holds a master of science in leisure studies from Central Missouri State University, and a PhD in curriculum and instruction: adult learning and development from the University of Missouri-Kansas City. Cathi has done post-doctoral work in environmental studies through Southern Illinois University.

In 1982, she experienced the sudden death of her first husband, John Wayne Cackler, with whom she shared two children, Bree and Brady Cackler. As a dutiful single mother, Cathi cared for two small children and continued her graduate education. Several years later, Cathi and Steve met. After a year of long-distance courtship, they decided to marry in 1986, forming a blended family. To that happy union a third child, Bryce Henson Veazey, was born, completing their family. From time to time their blended family has been expanded by several stray animals. Cathi is a rescuer of domestic (and wild) animals that are in distress or lost.

"What Matters Most?" For Cathi it is not her educational achievements, volunteer work, ministry, and artistry. What matters most is her love for Steve, being an affectionate mother, mother-in-law, and grandmother that spends her time supporting her family an array of professional, entrepreneurial, and personal activities. When asked to describe Cathi, husband Steve said,

> "She is the rock of our family, always sacrificing her time and energies to support and care for family members. She is a very dedicated church member, minister, and leader. I could not serve as president of the church without her support and encouragement. Her extensive volunteer service to the community is an extension of her faith and sense of calling to be an agent of community building wherever she is. She has a keen, analytical mind and a kind, open heart, which is a unique combination. I enjoy her love of nature and her works of art tremendously. I am very fortunate and blessed that she is my lifelong companion."

Far More to This

It seems to me there's a leak.
Certitude keeps dripping away.
I don't know what I used to know.
I could quote scripture, spell hermeneutics,
    and unwrap mystical mysteries.
After all, God was my buddy and Jesus my friend.
They spoke to me and I arrogantly spoke for them.

"It SEEMS to me," has replaced, "THAT'S the way it IS!"
Mysteries dance daily in my mind:
    explore, release, renew, reclaim—so little firmly framed.
Queries birth queries. Assurance has no sway.
Omnipotence is not God's friend nor yours.
    Who walks on water with feet of clay?
Salvation is NOW, not then.
Salvation is you and I knowing when to say, "YES!"
    and when to say, "NO!"
It's forgiving, forgetting, and moving on.
It's erasing dividing lines.
It's divinity and humanity in harmony.
It probes the unknown, engages life questions
    —unlocks heads, hearts and souls.
It constantly creates what SHOULD be.
Faith is not signing on to what was.
Faith is hope's invitation to lean forward,
    improving what is and pursing what can be.
Theology, void of hands and feet, is the wording of faith
    minus the working of faith.
That's NOT the way it is!
Thankfully (it seems to me) someone or something
    keeps whispering,
"There's far more to this than you think you know!"

Awakening

Clouded by everydayness the awakening comes
    with sudden startling joy unbidden and all is stripped away.
Voices die within the mind, a "hemorrhaging of the soul,"[59]
    and only "NOW" can speak its name.
Its whisper felt, not heard, speaks warmth and tears and solitude,

for we are one and time stands mute.
The AWAKENING—free of fanfare's beating drums
    and traffic's absent swish and squeal, drowned in seas of silence.
A sudden flash of color—freeze-framed feathers on the wing.
The secret now unwrapped, winking its tiny light
    in my night of discovery.
A brief, fleeting glimpse of what "being" is
    —its deeper reality swallowed soon by circus acts
    and sleepy days of sameness.
It breathes but for a moment yet fills eternity—
    this soft, quiet time somewhere between
    what was, what is and what will be.
AWAKENING. Surrendering to the sublime NOW.
This, this, alone. So, short, yet long.
This singularity. This flood of love and life so soon asleep again.

Dare to Love

Venture forth beyond survival. Break the chains of safety's song.
Mute its chorus of protection. Dare to love and live Love's song.
    Dare to shed convention's garments; Dare to say what must be said.
    Dare to be a pilgrim people. Dare to journey paths yet tread.
Called to love without conditions. Called to love and pay love's price.
Dare to love and risk rejection. Dare to live the peace of Christ.
    Risk, O Church, your resurrection, boldly journey to the cross
    Where the death of indecision Liberates the least and lost.
Sleep no more in moderation; Shatter walls of segregation.
Welcome all without exception. Dare to love not counting cost.
    Time has passed for hesitation; Heed no more convention's view.
    Kneel, O, church, and make confession, be courageous, stand anew.
Stripped of pleasing condescension; dare to do what Christ would do.
Honor Love's diverse expressions. Dare to love as God loves you.
    Called to love without conditions. Called to love and pay love's price.
    Dare to love and risk rejection. Dare to live the peace of Christ.

Parochial Peace

Blindly at war with ourselves, we have weighed peace on humanity's scales.
We have measured its height, width, and length, and given it our blessing—
our "balm in Gilead" sprinkled on troubled waters, warring factions, and
wayward souls. Peace—wrapped so neatly and completely in daydreams

where hurts dissolve, worries die, food is plenty, and problems solved. A
never-never land of sunny days, lemonade, carefree breezes, and discount
prices. Humanity's parochial peace that sees no end to forests green and
waters clean of air to breathe and mountain streams of species rare no
longer seen. Parochial peace is promise poor and silently it wages war on
Mother Earth—our womb of life that moans and groans for liberty. Look not
to foreign lands and seas in search of her cruel enemies. They live within
each breath we take, each choice we make, each pledge we break to heal and
save the Earth—our wounded self that yearns for peace beyond our peace—a
peace that brings rebirth.

Getting Through[60]

How do I get through,
    using these frail fragile containers, God,
    these letters woven into words shortchanged of meaning?
Tired, overworked, always wanting,
    they carry that which cannot be carried:
    the joy and hurt of the heart's song that sleepy letters cannot sing.
My hopes, dreams, and deepest feelings escape utterance
    because the clothes don't fit.
They wrap themselves in hidden beauty.
Peeking, seeking, teasing, like a childhood game
    their meaning unannounced by sayings, sounds,
    and soft winds of scattered thoughts.
So much unclaimed, unheard, unrealized.
Prayer without wings. Breath without air.
And yet, despite my wordless cries
You are deep inside and hear me.

When Faith is Thin

There are days when silence mutes each hopeful song's refrain,
    and absence shouts that God's asleep, and courage has no name.
But not this day—for on this day the Spirit brings release,
    and wings my wounded soul aloft on winds that never cease.
There are days when questions loom that drain belief away,
    and darkness shrouds the morning's dawn till sunlight has no sway.
But not this day—for on this day the Spirit brings release
    and lifts the burdens of self-doubt that tether faith's increase.
There are days when faith is thin, and failure calls my name
    when sorrow sings its lonely song, and prayers ascend in vain.

But not this day—for on this day the Spirit brings release
  and fills my empty soul again with blessings of Christ's peace.
There are days when all seems lost, yet I am not alone
  amid the swirling dance of doubt the Spirit wings me home.
The One who fills the starry night with orbs of pulsing light
  sustains the smallest bird in flight and calms each raging storm.

Forever Young

Bells ring. Doors open. Sneakers. "Skechers." Sandals. T-shirts. Blue jeans. Bandanas. Laughter. Chatter. Lockers cleaned and clanged. Middle school cacophony. Giggles, pigtails, and bright shiny faces screaming down hallways. Then suddenly, silence. Emptiness. A sea of classmates gone. All but one, God—lingering behind, standing, waiting—his gaze fixed on Room 101. His room. Their room. For the fourth time, in as many minutes, he shrugs, prepares to leave, then stops, tosses "Captain America" over his shoulder crammed with books, pens, two sweaty tees, and somewhere, a crumbled picture of Ashley that will not survive the ride home, let alone summer.

Summer! Sweet summer! Sleep-in summer! Lazy, hazy days. Camp, baseball, hot days, and hot dogs. Sun, sand, wind and waves. Forever young! Forever fun. Not for him. Not for Ashley. Not for Karl, Mateo, "Digger," Andréa, Winston, LaKeisha, Mr. Duncan, and four others, critically wounded. Room 101. Less than 20 seconds, God. 400 rounds per minute, God. Eight bloodied targets, who are now 'forever young,' God! Rallies. Protests. Teenage pleas and eloquent speeches. A million signs. A million tears. A million "thoughts and prayers" and broken promises—and "Never Again" becomes again, again, and AGAIN!

When, will children be valued more than bullets?
When will "Nothing can be done" become "THY WILL be done?"
When will parents' cries penetrate political deafness?
When will collective courage defeat collective silence?
When will love of life exceed love of profit?
When will students no longer huddle in supply rooms, hide beneath
  desks, hear the clatter of gunfire, taste terror, see shattered flesh
  and bones, weep for friends?
When will children, "Never Again" remain forever young?
  Only when we make it so! God help us!

Ḣer Ḣeart, An Open Door
Sandra Ann Fielder

Sandra Ann Fielder slipped away peacefully on December 11, 2013, at the age of 62 after a courageous battle against cancer. She faced death as she faced life—filled with abiding faith in her God, loving devotion for her husband and best friend, her children, grandchildren, extended family, and unknowingly—a host of persons whose lives were transformed by her vibrant presence and kindness. Sandra saw herself as an ordinary person, but many graced to know her were touched indelibly by her extraordinary love for life and her compassion for disadvantaged souls. She and her husband, Terry, welcomed me in their home and their hearts more than thirty years ago during the early years of my ministry in Northern, Ontario, Canada.

Sandra met her life partner and best friend, Terry, in kindergarten. She married at nineteen and set aside her planned teaching career a year and a half later when the first of their four children arrived. Terry amusingly contends that their "Four Ts" (Tyandra, Tyler, Terra, and Trisha) arrived in advance of Terry and Sandra's planned parenting calendar.

Sandra invested herself in making this world a better place, especially for children. No lines were drawn—son, daughter, grandchild, student or the kid next door—every child was her child. She was a teacher in the classroom, Sunday school, and life. She took pride in others' successes and supported them in their struggles. She followed a healthy and active lifestyle. Sandra lived very much in the moment; she was so engrossed with what was happening in the "now" her friends joked about her challenge to arrive to meetings on time. She was always worth waiting for, and she sometimes surprised her amused critics by arriving early.

Terry managed their Home Hardware Store while Sandra (a lifelong learner) earned two university degrees and several diplomas. She returned to her teaching career shortly after Terry became the first director of World Accord, an international community-development agency. His work included raising funds across Canada for programs primarily in Latin America and Asia. As director, he traveled widely (often accompanied by Sandra) working together with those in need.

Sandra was forever eager to gain insights from international travel, her give-and-take with students, her church family, and from those lacking formal schooling whose wisdom trumped academia. From mountain villages to her church, home, classroom and community, she was a teacher powered by faith and the desire to reflect God's love to others. Sandra was incredibly adept at helping children with reading difficulties. She made reading fun and exciting, unfolding new worlds of "self-learning" that enabled children in wanting circumstance to be set free.

Terry, the "Four Ts," their spouses, and six grandchildren decided not to memorialize Sandra's death annually but to celebrate her birthday. For the Fielder family, birth and beginnings trump endings. Grief is love's invoice—an invoice Terry will continue to pay because love is not eclipsed by death's shadow. In Sandra's words, *"Don't cry because it's over; smile because it happened."*

Reflection: Greater Than Self

In our better moments, we respond to love's call by placing ourselves in harm's way for others. Police officers shot on duty, firemen charging into flaming infernos, soldiers scrambling to save colleagues, and so-called "ordinary people" unhesitatingly laying down their lives for complete strangers. Heroism is seldom, if ever, a matter of intellectual debate. Fear, and risk fly out the window. In a sense, *the act of saving another is an act of saving oneself.* Life is co-dependent and co-joined. *I am you; you are me; we are one.* At points of mutual crises, our "oneness" echoes, "Do unto others as you would have them do unto you." (John 3:16). Self-sacrifice, however, is not the ultimate expression of love when viewed through the lens of the doctrine of Christian atonement.

What does atonement mean? What does Christ's death on a cross have to do with our being forgiven, accepted, and loved? Have we fashioned a god whose "priceless love" is not priceless? How does atonement square with unconditional love? Have the ancient creeds rendered the gospel transactional? *"There is no recorded saying of Jesus in which he explicitly connects his death with the forgiveness or remission of sins."*[61] One wonders at the feeding of five thousand with five loaves and two fish? One wonders did Jesus walk on water, calm the storm, restore sight, heal lepers? One wonders why your sin and mine is nailed to the cross of Jesus when the remedy for sin throughout the Hebrew Bible (the Old Testament) was forgiveness. I applaud Leslie D. Weatherhead's liberating statement, *"Where in the Gospels are we ever told that Christ demanded belief in some theological proposition before he would admit a seeker into his discipleship? The answer is that he never did."*[62]

Atonement generally is understood as the penultimate length, width, and depth of God's love. "For God so loved the world that he gave his only Son"—John3: 16. Frankly, the concept of sacrificing one's child to atone for another is anathema to any parent. Could I lay down my life for another? I honestly don't know. Could I do so for my wife or a daughter? Yes, without question! Could I sacrifice one of my daughters for the life of another? Never! Atonement theories (the Ransom theory, Satisfaction theory, Substitution theory, Moral influence theory, etc.) run counter to the concept of grace, itself.

If one rejects the concept of Christ's atonement is there anything redeemable (no pun intended) in this unconscionable doctrine? Yes, ironically because it is "unconscionable." When taken *figuratively*, rather than *literally*, the quixotic atonement narrative shatters traditional boundaries of what we think to be love's ultimate expression, namely, "self-sacrifice."

When we literalize biblical narratives, we disempower them. Metaphorically, Christian atonement (criticized by some as the epitome of child abuse) is "theo-poetics"—a shocking, parabolic, narrative—that pushes love beyond moral comprehension. It proffers a reprehensible paradox where competing moral values are outrageously turned upside down and inside-out; it *hyperbolizes* the length, depth, and breadth of divine love, by positing the repugnant trespass of a line too unthinkable to cross. Love limited becomes its own enemy.

Theoretically, atonement (if nothing else) pushes us beyond rational packaged answers. It reminds us that we are not the pinnacle of creation. It reminds us that this life of wonder, chaos, joy, hope, pain, and renewal is an ongoing process of "AT-ONE-MENT." We are here. We are ONE. We are flawed, failing, living, dying, sharing, giving—at one with each other, the stars above, the grass beneath our feet. We are living breathing stardust equally loved amid the chaos and blessing of living. There is something greater than self.

One Note

A single dot upon the staff. Humanity's one note serendipitously added to the score: God's evolutionary "Fanfare of the Fittest," consistently amending, appending, obliterating, conceiving, and playing its music through ages undeterred. Before time had name or measure, creation hummed its melody—

chaos mixed with harmony—unaided by humanity's solitary sound. And what a sound it was and is. Self-inflated. Self-absorbed. Singing and soaring above creation's symphony—or so it seems. So late upon the scene we scream our one-note song precluding and excluding all that sings before, above, within, without. Forgive our arrogance, God. Our fractured independence. Our center-stage conceit wallowing in the spotlight of self-aggrandizement.

For Such a Time, as This

For such a time, as this, we kneel and pray
 and sing our thanks for food, for friends, for family,
 for shelter from the winds of war
 that rage within the purest heart when evil has its way.
Newborns sleep in alleyways and cry for milk
 from empty breasts. Young men die in sandy dunes,
 and oil is valued more than blood.
Arms are mapped by needle tracks
 and twelve-year-olds are sold for sex and never see the sun.
For such a time, as this, we raise our eyes
 and clap our hands and dance the dance of politics
 where promises of softer times, of safety and security,
 of healthcare, and prosperity are spun by campaign victories
 and sealed by smiling lips—until the oath is taken.
For such a time, as this, we search for God in hallowed halls
 and temple spires, in worn-out pews and homespun choirs,
 in gospel bands with giant screens that save our souls
 with PowerPoint, till Monday comes again.
For such a time, as this, we look beneath
 our shades of skin and see within that we are kin,
 that whirling dance and pentagrams,
 prayer mats, mosques, and epigrams
 of holy writ, whose sacred scripts declare that we are one.
For such a time, as this, our hearts proclaim
 that love is not a gender game, that beauty paints each child the same,
 that every soul shares equal worth, that we are but the thinking earth,
 that trees and grass and mountain streams permeate our very birth.
We are blessed beyond compare
 and heaven greets us everywhere, in every face,
 in every breeze, in every soaring melody,
 in morning's light and silent night,
 in stars that shine, in hope that sings, in every drop of dancing rain,
 the whisper of Love's sweet refrain:
 "My peace I give unto you, for such a time, as this."

Cathedral

Whirling. Swirling. Skyward.
Here, in this sacred space, we sense your Spirit, God,
not because where we walk, talk,
and live our daily lives are less sacred.
Every sanctuary: large, small, humble or ornate
—every living room, field, forest, mountain stream
awakens us to your presence.
We come expectant. We come in search of you,
in search of ourselves, of those we know and do not know
who need to be blessed and be a blessing.
How many have walked the Worshiper's Path?
How many faces, races, friends, families, strangers?
Heads bowed in silence, hearts filled with hope and anticipation.
Upward. Inward. Slowly, reflectively,
winding their way into swirling sacred space.
Bringing you there, meeting you there—taking you with them.

The Scars Remain

The following cathartic response to 9/11 was saved, hidden, and forgotten on my computer. That fateful morning, Americans wept, and the human family tasted salt. Tragedy has power to unite us. The insanity of school shootings spill into our living-rooms unabated, whose victims are close as next door. Innocent children ripped from the arms of weeping mothers and fathers at our borders vicariously become our children. Pain slowly dissipates, but scars remain.

Decades slip away and still the scars remain. Three thousand dreams un-
tasted, three thousand hopes undone. Tumbling, crumbling towers rise
skyward once again descending ever downward fueled by memory's flame.
Who? What? Why and When? replay their silent songs in rhythms sad and
searing scared by death's dark hand.

Bursts of winged inferno repeated one by one. Death's billowing cloud of
flaming ash, of fiery flesh and bone shroud life's light in shadows deep that
cease to dissipate. Sister, brother, parent, child—baker, banker, order-taker—
young and old no more shall age. Airborne heroes scattered in the soil.
Friends in hallways scorched away. Cell phone calls. Short goodbyes:
"I love you!" dropped and done.

Still the scars remain for all whose lives are knit to theirs by love's eternal
flame. And what of we who have no claim to they whose lives are gone—who
from afar saw images replayed from dusk to dawn? Who wept for names we
never knew and faces never seen and braced the fierce reality that innocence
was gone?

The holy hands that shape us are not God's alone. Beyond assumed divinity
we touch each other's soul—smooth, rough, calloused, delicate and delicious
—molding, unfolding, forming and informing all we've been, all we are, all
we may become. And what have we become within the sweep of space? What
future lies before us, beyond this time and place? What lessons have we
failed to learn, what give and take remains? In honor of those fallen, can
retribution cease? Can hands reach out to bridge the gap when violence
severs peace? Forgive? Forget? Release? Reset? Begin a brand-new day?
So long ago, so far away—and still the scars remain—for we have dried a
million tears that love has drained away.

Reflection: When Belief Becomes Biography

Theology/ideology becomes biography for bane or blessing. We become like the god or gods we worship. If your god is angry and unforgiving, you will be angry and unforgiving. The same principle applies to the non-religious. Whatever prime directive (moral or otherwise) they choose to follow will shape who they are and who they become.

I can neither authenticate nor adequately describe the *Abiding Presence, Deeper Reality or "Principle of Rightness*[63]*"* to which I respond. Despite humanity's unbridled ecological degradation and chronic acts of inhumanity I choose to believe goodness exceeds evil. Famine, drought, earthquake, wind and fire are not punishments of a petulant deity. Sunshine surpasses storms. I celebrate a cosmology that sparks the birth of stars as well as the death of galaxies. I marvel at spiraling chains of DNA that determine blue eyes, blonde hair—an athlete, artist, poet or prodigy—the height, weight, shape and maximum lifetime of children yet born. I choose to believe *reality* is predominately benevolent.

This choice is of course, subjective. It is embedded and emotively fueled more by hope than logic or reason. It is a personal verdict flooded by oceans of optimism surging from family, friends, teachers, preachers and drenched by serendipitous waves of kindnesses from unexpected people and sources. Taught and caught it resides deep in the marrow of who I am. A fool's choice? Perhaps. A Pollyannaish faith that will not let me go despite the abyss of unknowing? Perhaps. A victory of *heart* over *head*—a subconscious refusal to *wholly abandon* supernatural theism? Ouch! Nonetheless, *I choose to believe life IS sacred* regardless of its disastrous dealings and disguises. Hope leans forward and so do I.

The Meaning of Friendship
Gary McDonald

"Literature, painting, music—the most basic lesson that all art teaches us is to stop, look, and listen to life on this planet, including our own lives, as a vastly richer, deeper, more mysterious business than most of the time it ever occurs to us to suspect as we bumble along from day to day on automatic pilot. In a world that for the most part steers clear of the whole idea of holiness, art is one of the few places left where we can speak to each other of holy things."
—Frederick Buechner.

"Integrity" immediately comes to mind when I think of Gary McDonald. It is not a virtue he has sought or claimed but one that has claimed him; it is simply, who he is. Gary is an extremely talented artist, poet, brilliant thinker, speaker, humorist, carpenter, "Mr. Fixit," and theologian. I am convinced though not seminary trained, he easily could pass a master of divinity or doctor of ministry examination. (I can hear him denying this!) His broad interests are rooted deeply in his hunger for knowledge, kinship with nature, and love for life. He is my muse and encourager ("pusher"), who reignited my interest in drawing and painting.

Gary is a successful Canadian artist whose paintings have been displayed at the Federation Gallery on Granville Island in Vancouver; the Tutt Gallery in Kelowna, British Columbia, Canada and in several Federation of Canadian Artists juried shows in the South Surrey/White Rock areas. Sales of his works and commissions continue to escalate, as does his reputation as an accomplished and sought-after artist. I keep reminding him as he ascends to greatness to "remember the little people." It is futile advice. Gary's humility is incurable.

Gary is the kindest, highest-principled, most caring person I know. He would throw his back out to avoid stepping on a June bug and never hesitates to help friend and stranger alike. I am convinced Gary's DNA contains genetic markers passed from a lapsed Dalia Lama. To sum it up, Gary is one with his word and his words are "trust," "honesty," "compassion," "dependability," "self-sacrifice" and, "integrity" (to name a few). He will consider this profile as "shameless deification," which attests to one of his greatest qualities: humility.

Artist's Song

I have wrapped you in wonder, and you have not seen. Earth, wind, sun, moon, and stars are cupped within my hand. I paint each season with life's hope. I sculpt each grain of sand. And yet my song remains unsung. Be my voice, my hands, my feet. Sketch my heart and soul. Speak for those who dare not speak. Stand for those who cannot stand. Be my balm, my healing touch, my oil of consecration, A smile, a listening ear, a word of hope, the gift of love's expression.

High Notes

Hope in a bottle and red-carpet lives. A minute or two of fame and fortune. An unwillingness to blend into the nothingness of the crowd. A chance to stand out, sing your song, feel the warmth of the spotlight, the applause of the crowd. Better yet, adoration from your peers—they who can assess your skills because they've been there—walked, stumbled, got up, dusted themselves off, found another hill to climb and did so successfully. I'm still climbing, tilting at windmills. Searching. Straining. "Dazzle us," you say? Sorry, I can't. Besides, I'm comfortable where I am. Well, not completely. I haven't arrived, by any stretch of the imagination. You know this, God. It's just that hope doesn't live in bottles and formulas and red carpets fade. Blending in isn't so bad. More of us need to. Life isn't competition; it's community—a celebration of diversity amid glorious harmony—an ability to hear everyone's unique song and say. "Well done!"—even if they didn't hit all the high notes.

Friendship

Friendship: The finding of self within another, unadorned, stripped clean of want or need. The naked self, shaped and shapeless, flawed and failing, never cast away. Encompassed. Embraced. Accepted. Respected. The board swept clean, the pieces tossed aside; the game "Who You Should Be" never played. For love's light seeks no victor; it glows within life's aches, seeps within the cracks and floods the soul with joy. Friendship: The giving of self to another, undemanding, unrestrained, unafraid. A dance of give and take— not counting cost—each leading, then following. Listening. Whispering. Gently reframing. Wisdom's caring voice. Silence in the storm. Sheer "presence" always enough. Blessed and blessing, a mutual knitting of souls.

The Painting

I'm painting now, God. Watercolors.
So, unforgiving, so surprising, rising
into accidental beauty here and there,
then gone again with blooms and brushes
and backwash hues unintended, or befriended.
A mixture of fun and frustration.
Torn masterpieces better left undone,
untouched by that one last added tone
unneeded, unheeded, depleted.
It's so hard to run before one walks.
Sistine Chapel dreams dancing with stick figures
in garish blue blobs.
Abstract excuses, "I meant it that way" plays only to the crowd,
while skin-tones streaked in stark orange shades
scream to be feathered, blended, not bruised.
Enough about me.
I love what you've done with the constellations, God.
A lot of space to work with, mind you.
But, ah, those shimmering backgrounds
—blue, black, velvet—swimming into nothingness,
shattered by purple spinning nebulae,
wispy gaseous sprays of matter straining to be born.
Wet on wet, or wet on dry? How do you keep doing it, God?
Nothing repeated. Colors that have no name,
blades of grass and hummingbird wings
splashed to perfection.
A hint of pink, a dab of New Gamboge,

a million shades of sunlight in a single grain of sand.
How many works have you tossed away?
Meanwhile, Old Masters hang on lofty walls
   with crowds for their pleasing—their ghostly creators weeping,
      "One's best is not enough." Never, never, enough.
Do you give lessons, God?
Is it ART, or are you just playing? How trite.
   You are the painting, aren't you?

Fault Line

Beneath my iffy beliefs and fleeting hopes, faith's fault line never sleeps.
Rumbling here then there, its troubled dance divides my head and heart
   —hiding, shifting, shaking, awakening
   questions posed, and answers sought.
While dreams of feathered angels' wings soar far beyond veracity
   in search of simple certitude stamped sure
   by childlike psalms and prayers that push the dark away.
Astride this deep divide, each foot a world apart,
I fix my gaze on treasured times when wonder ruled my heart.
Sweet memories of mysteries of miracles and fantasies,
   of words and deeds and prophesies
   —where crumbs of bread and drops of wine
   cupped within Love's healing hands
   spun promises of pearly gates, a Neverland of joy and peace
   for lion, lamb, and child.
But comfort's kiss of yesterday is fleeting and benign
   and sacredness cannot be bound by magic's sleight of hand.
Foundations deeply shaken by probing of the mind
   have silenced songs of make-believe
   and stirred within my revelry the witness of eternity:
   the Spirit breathes beyond our creeds, and Love is not a dream.
Stripped clean of measured litanies, of strained beliefs and fantasies,
   the mystic will not die.
Faith's whispered invocation
   forever calls my name.

"Many an atheist is a believer without knowing it just as many a believer is an atheist without knowing it. You can sincerely believe there is no God and live as though there is. You can sincerely believe there is a God and live as though there isn't."[64] —Frederic Buechner

An Agnostic's Prayer

I believe in the ocean's breeze—the kiss of salt upon my lips,
*   the whistling wind through rustling leaves,*
*   the sting of winter's biting breeze.*
I believe in life and death and all that lies between
—sheer ecstasies and agonies birthed by choice and whim.
I believe in love and hate in lessons learned and fickle fate
*   where hurts and healings take their place*
*   amid the dance of circumstance. But ask me not to pray.*
No head to bow, no knees to kneel, no hands to fold, no silent words
*   with hushed appeals for miracles or magic things to serve my needs*
*   or save my soul. It's mine alone, you see.*
The wondering, the wandering, the tempo of my passing days
*   are filled with all that comes my way—a dance of joy or pain.*
I ask no more than life affords. I give myself to honesty, integrity,
*   good company and helping where I may. But I'm unsure of sacred things,*
*   the meaning and the mystery that puts my life in play. I have not found*
*   this god of gods—the Source of All, you say. I hear no voice. I see no*
*   face, no spirit ecstasy and yet, I fellowship with those who do,*
*   but ask me not to pray.*

An Atheist's Prayer

A fortuitous concourse of atoms, protons, electrons, quanta, particles and waves, whatever—bubbling up the soup of life. Big Bang? Small Bang? Either way there's nobody's name on it. Just the luck of the draw. Look, I know the odds—the improbable delicate balance that keeps it all in play—the infinitesimal intricacies of physics holding life in its hands. We're a hair's breadth from non-existence. Quite a balancing act, but there's nobody's name on it. So, I dance my dance free of a grand composer, with just my name on it. Mine and all who choose their own music. I believe in goodness for goodness's sake. I believe in joy, hope, love, and peace. I believe in community, fairness, justice, kindness, honesty, truthfulness, generosity. And, yes, I believe in the human spirit that tells me each person has worth. We separate, segregate and castigate the least, the lost, the labeled and seek to save our own. I believe we're all one family and have forgotten our names. I believe we owe our planet a living and fail to give it one. I believe we can do better and I'll gladly put my name on it. Amen

Measured Gaze

"Beauty got in the way, like a thick cobweb through which it was difficult to see her clearly"[65]—Robert Gailbreath. a.k.a. J. K. Rowling

Beauty self-defined holds sway
*   on face and form of all we meet and greet;*
*   their splendor squeezed by rubrics we've assigned.*
The curve of a cheek, cupid lips,
*   deep-set eyes drowned in speckled blues and browns.*
Made-to-measure beauty—elective, selective, hiding, abiding.
Designer clothes demanding thin lines, tiny waists,
*   swelling breasts, legs that have no end.*
Slinky shadowed silhouettes few can cast or carry.

Tanned physic, chiseled chin, perpetual stubble,
*   twitching pecks, rippling abs, shocks of spiked hair.*
*   "In or out?" "Pass or fail?"—a fleeting glance determined.*
Wrinkles be damned. Gray is black.
Sagging jowls, waggly waddles neatly sliced away.
Beauty—painted plastic, a nip and tuck, botoxed brows,
*   a symmetry of shallowness that hides what lies within.*

The masses quickly cast aside;
*   bushy eyebrows, bulbous nose, twisted smiles,*
*   thinning hair, too short, too stout, too tall, too thin*
*   —a fate far worse than death.*
Swallowed by their plainness.
"Me-too" souls somewhere in the background
*   —unengaged, unwrapped, unknown,*
*   brilliant, and blessed*
How many have I written off?
What beauty have my eyes dismissed?
What wisdom, friendship, pure delight
*   dies beneath my measured gaze?*

Songbird
Helene McDonald

Listening. Loving. Keeping. When you share in conversation with Helene McDonald she listens intently, discerning what is said and unsaid, with the promise of unwavering confidentiality. If the lyrics "Knowing what to throw away and knowing what to keep" from singer, Kenny Roger's "The Gambler" apply to anyone, it is Helene. She discards all divisive categories of status by honoring the worth of all persons while holding firmly to high ethical standard that govern her life.

A gifted artisan in her own right, Helene puts professional gardeners and interior decorators to shame. She has exquisite taste, a designer's eye, and intuitively knows what accessory goes well with what and where. She instinctively discerns which window, wall or ceiling cries for alteration. A blessing for her—a burden for "make-it-happen Gary."

SONGBIRD? Yes! I have saved the best for last! Helene has the most beautiful soprano voice, I have been privileged to hear. Having performed leading roles with the Vancouver Opera, Helene's vocals do not flow from a composer's page, conductor's baton or the grandeur of chorus and orchestra. Helene does not give a performance. Helene gives herself. She is the music that soars effortlessly, softly, strongly, and emotively from the depths of who she is whether in operatic character or as guest soloist. (Is it all right to have a crush on your best friend's wife? Sure, it is!) I can hear Helene denying everything I have said. I also can hear Gary saying, 'Halya' (her Ukrainian name) don't argue with him! He's right!"

Songbird

The songbird sings her joyous song with feathers freed,
  no longer bound to earthly chains that held her down.
She sings and soars on windswept wings
  and sails above deep-shadowed shores that trapped her soul within.
Upward! Outward! Inward! Free to climb the sky again,
  to seek the sun and breathe again,
  to dance the dance of joy again
  where blessings of life's simple things, are once again reborn.
Sweet mysteries untouched, unclaimed,
  unwrapped amid the winds of change
  are seen with newfound sight.
With outstretched wing and beating pulse
  through rhythmic sweep of soundless space
  she swirls in freedom's flight.
Laughter is her melody. Spirit is her song.
She floats on wings of faith and grace
  with hope her constant view, for even in the darkest night,
  the songbird sings anew.

Only Helene's inward beauty surpasses her physical beauty. Helene is forthright, intelligent, thought provoking, forgiving, insightful, and gracious. Her ethos is beyond question. I never have heard her negatively critique another, and confidentiality, for Helene, is an impenetrable, sacred trust.

Reflection: The Re-animation of Wonder

Praise (religious and otherwise) reawakens one's sense of "being." Whether believer, agnostic or atheist, the sheer wonder of life cannot go unacknowledged. Praise through formal worship or awakened by a sea-kissed sunset is not exclusively externally enlivened but arises from an inward experience of awe. Praise is not hostage to knee-bent supplications or sanctuaries. In its broadest sense, praise is re-animation of wonder; a bright shining moment of aliveness that discards self-centeredness in lieu of a higher, more pressing claim—pure joy for life and renewed gratitude for all that sustains it. We experience anamnesis—a lively awareness that the present is suddenly freed from countless voices that mercilessly vie for our attention. Juxtaposition of yesterday's failures and victories remind us we have come through life's highs and lows. Whatever joy, pain, or sorrow the future holds—love, trust, and hope can see us through tomorrow.

We frequently take life for granted instead of with gratitude. Routine robs us of being fully alive. We can be so caught up in the way things are; we forget how things once were and how much better things can be. Life is not a solo act; its tapestry is multifaceted. We are woven together by diverse threads neither less than nor greater than the evolving fabric of the cosmos. The invoice of this reality is humility and thanksgiving. It comes due frequently far afield from liturgical acts and stained-glass windows.

The heartbeat of irrepressible praise is unfettered thankfulness. Ultimately, praise reminds us that humanity is not the pinnacle of creation. Despite self-inflated attempts to unwrap life's mysteries, someone or something—a Deeper Reality—enlivens all that is. Worship's purpose is not to praise or placate this Deeper Reality or Creative Presence. In traditional verbiage, praise is not for God's benefit; it is for our benefit. Divine "applause" declares we are codependent on each other, on every wispy cloud, twinkling star, and blade of grass. Whether acknowledged or taken for granted, we stand constantly in the presence of GREATNESS. Failing to applaud this WONDER, whether at the office desk, workbench, playing field, or pew is to cheat one's self and life itself.

Beyond Choice

Helene's giving of herself (on stage and off) is a principle of life so part of her that it is beyond conscious choice. Such personal life commandments arise from a conviction that something (someone?) is far greater than self. The following considers what stirs within us when awakened to this reality.

Clapping hands, red, raw, burning!
Stinging applause drowned in seas of unbridled praise
    wave upon wave unrestrained.
Thunderous, wondrous, unstoppable!
More than standing ovation. More than adulation.
More than praise for composition, props, and lighting,
    soloists, swelling chorus, singing strings,
    blaring brass or symbol.
To not applaud is my soul's indictment.
To not applaud cheats all that is:
    musician, stagehand, audience,
    the air I breathe, the ground beneath my feet.
A fleeting bright awakening!
Applause beyond choice, praising that which causes all to be
    —the very core of wonder's source.
In the presence of greatness, we can do no other.

Priorities

Time marches on. Not for some, God.
It runs like a race-horse or crawls like an ant.
We yearn to turn back the clock
Buff bodies, botoxed brows, and collagen lips.
Designer jeans ripped and torn at Cadillac prices
     —old before their time.
The look is young, tattered, and text-messaged.
So where do we old-timers fit in? What's real and not-real
     in this "special-effects" world?
Are you with it, God? Can you keep up? It all seems so digital.
Everybody counts, or nobody counts
     in a culture drunk with individualism and celebrity
     while millions die with HIV and countless starve.
Everyone's important—the litany goes,
     though some more so than others.
Endless loops of TV news of who's kissing who,
     who's in rehab, and who's lost weight
     —sprinkled with a liberal dose of suicide bombers
     and singing contests. Right! It's all been said before,
     "We're going to hell in hand basket!"
Evangelicals wonder when you're going to show up, Jesus
Surely, when you come you'll be sporting brand new jeans
     —no tears, no holes, no fraying—just praying that when you speak
     you won't need to be translated.

Somewhere In-between

Somewhere in-between feathered faith and knowing, truth's aching, straining
songs of Spirit sing siren melodies of hope that all has not seeped away
between fact and fantasy. Somewhere in-between knowing and not wanting to
know—between belief's untimely death and faith's wounded resurrection—the
the fog of unbelief dissipates and seeks what cannot be sought: faith's final
dispensation—where magic dies and mystery grants no keys to doubt's
undoing. A letting go. A glinging to. A dance yet undecided. The rhythm
changed, the movement strange, the floor forever rising. Each step unsure, I
stumble forth with wispy words of mystical truths discarded, yet undying.

Kindness, Dedication, Service
Bob and Diane Kyser

Bob and Diane Kyser's Christian discipleship is not "in word only" (1 Thessalonians 1:5 NRSV). Their passion to help others is as natural as breathing. They do not consider themselves special or extraordinary. Their kindness, dedication and service to those in need, witness otherwise. Bob and Diane's unique individual strengths stand on their own merit but are amplified when combined together.

Bob officially retired from a ministerial career spanning thirty years of service. I say, "officially," because Bob never will fully retire from ministry. He serves in leadership roles in his home congregation and in various volunteer capacities for his denomination's International Headquarters.

Bob has not only served his church, but his country. Following graduate studies at The George Washington University in Washington, DC, Bob served the US Army for a two-year term during the Vietnam War. Basic training was challenging (he was jokingly told he was "too old") but was a life experience he later felt could not be replaced.

He re-enlisted for an extended period, which led to additional training and a specialization as a German linguist. Being stationed in Augsburg, Germany, provided Bob and Diane the opportunity to see *Europe on 5 Dollars a Day* (a popular travel book title of the time). Bob helped develop communications intelligence for various military exercises and was part of a unit tasked with intercepting communications from a well-known terrorist gang.

Germany provided opportunity for Bob and Diane to expand their appreciation of their church as a worldwide organization. They formed relationships that have lasted a life time. Bob preached his first sermon in German, shared in the church's annual family camp, and attended the annual US military church members retreat.

Bob always had a desire to follow in his father's footsteps as a minister. In Bob's earlier life, this did not seem possible, but opportunity to realize this dream came to fruition when he was a missionary minister for Community of Christ. Inviting people into a deeper relationship with Christ, helping congregations grow, planting new congregations, encouraging people to share stories of God in their lives were his passions lived through assignments in the United States and Latin America.

Teaming with others, Bob produced several missionary resources. He worked with others to produce "Gospel Wagon Ministries," designed to equip children to become disciples of Jesus. He also expanded the role of the "Young Peacemakers Club," helping children gain skills in following Christ's model of peacemaking. After retirement he formed a team to create a children's spiritual formation center for his home congregation. Bob continues to contribute his gift of teaching and preaching ministry to his congregation and beyond. Bob not only is a "fisher of men, women, and children," he also "casts his net on the other side" as an avid fisherman!

Bob's retirement motto is "Living the GAP!" (Grandfather, Adventure, Presence ministry). In response to this post-career goal, he and Diane have served as a World Service Corps team in New Zealand (where Diane's father was born, and her grandparents were an early missionary family focused on ministry with the indigenous Maori people) and Europe .

Diane has pursued peace as a pioneer in the field of mediation, reconciliation, and restorative justice for more than thirty years. She has a master's degree in physical education from Indiana University, and a master's degree in conflict transformation from Eastern Mennonite University. She established a mediation center in Davenport, Iowa, and served as its executive director for nine years. Bob's job brought them to Independence, Missouri, where in 1999 Diane, established the Community Mediation Center in Independence, Missouri, and served as its executive director. The center serves the citizens of metropolitan Kansas City and the surrounding counties, providing conflict-resolution training, facilitation, consultation, and mediation services.

Diane has provided training for businesses, organizations, schools, and churches, and has taught Peace Studies classes at Park University and Graceland University. She has managed mediation programs for small-claims court, municipal court, circuit court, and family court. She also served as chair of Community of Christ's peace and justice committee for twenty years and continues to discover ways to engage people in peaceful methods of conflict resolution. While she might have chosen a career path in politics, law, or education, Diane chose rather to be a peacemaker—one life, one set of relationships at a time. Her passion to bless the lives of others has never waned and continues to find new expressions of fulfillment in retirement.

Diane's motto, (borrowed from somewhere, she claims) is: *"Achieving world peace—one conflict at a time."* She advocates that practical steps toward peace are achieved in helping people address the conflicts of their daily lives in respectful, cooperative ways such that relationships can be whole. Bob and Diane's life and ministry easily can be wrapped-up in three words: love, kindness, and witness.

Bob and Diane refuse to label people; every soul is of inestimable worth. These two-exceptional people share life as a team devoted to each other and the call "Toward Zion for all!" I have no doubt the coming chapters of their story will be the most exciting of all.

"We have always been amazed in our own deeper reflections that two so very different people might engage in life's journey together. Perhaps the key has been our mutual affirmation of each other's uniqueness while blending our common passions into life's goals. One of our overriding goals is the pursuit of zionic community in which the value and equality of each person may be lived in peace and justice for all."

Toward Humility

We've fed the hungry. Dropped change in a beggar's bowl.
Uttered prayers. Sung hymns. Paid tithes.
We have studied and prepared. We have held hands of the sick,
broken bread, blessed wine, shared love's words
 across pulpits, board rooms, and lunch counters.
We have blessed and been blessed.
Hear now our confession, Lord:
 for we have warmed ourselves
 at the hearth of praise and bask in light meant for you.
Idleness and apathy have called our name.
Forgive our self-indulgence. Strip away our self-sufficiency.
Restore your Spirit within us.
Let humility illumine the wonder of servanthood
 that we might hear your word of hope and speak it,
 see injustice and correct it, feel pain and relieve it,
 share love and live it.

Never Cheap

Goodness is expensive! We give it away in various shapes and sizes, but there's always a cost. A mite or a million. Every deed exacts a price: a pat on the back, a passing smile, a wallet returned, a door opened, a note of "thanks," a warm handshake, a nod of forgiveness, a slate wiped clean, And love? How expensive is love? A garden retreat, a kiss on the cheek, a trial, a cross, an empty tomb, another bright resurrection morning—this morning! Every morning. Grace! Costly! Never cheap! Yet always stamped: "Paid in full!" No "this for that!" Just THIS! The good news of living the right arrangement of relationships! At what cost? Humility: the high price of receiving without earning. Grace pursues us in all its disguises (sacred or secular) yet never renders an invoice.

Music of the Moral Universe

Text, tune, notes on a staff, rising, descending, holding on, letting go.
"The fourth, the fifth, the minor fall, the major lift."[66]
Sacred music: the songs of the moral universe
stir my soul and wakes my sleeping spirit.
Thank God, for this language of the soul
and those gifted to shape, sing, and compose it.
Songs of praise and adoration. Songs of doubt, desperation,
pleading, needing, seeking love's will and way.
Evolution's song plays on—birthing, dying, expanding, contracting,
discordant, disjunctive, chaotic and sweet.
God, you live in life's rhythms, its thrum and its beat, allegro,
andante, forever creating, never complete.
You creep with the infant, sleep in the street,
limp with the aged, leap with the young.
You're out there cavorting beyond chapel and song
beyond domed cathedral and swirling steel spire
where dry bones keep rising enflamed with love's fire!
You've smiled us into smiling God, laughed in our joy,
cried in our sorrow, danced in our hope.
You put us to sleep; resurrect us each dawn.
You carve our names on the palms of your hands,
place songs of hope, in our hearts, and our dreams.
May each note we play today be a symphony of grace.
May the prayers we offer grant release—a healing touch
a listening ear, an open heart—a table of fellowship
where all are accepted and sing their own song.

Reflection: Another You and Me?

William Cleary, in his book, *Prayer to an Evolutionary God* says, "We are each a part of something larger than ourselves—how large we can only guess."[67] "Science," said Einstein, "without religion is lame; religion without science is blind."[68] Pierre Teilhard de Chardin adds the spiritual note: "Neither in its impetus nor its achievements can science go to its limits without becoming tinged with mysticism."[69] Science seeks to unfold the mysteries of physics while theology, in Anselm's words, is "faith seeking understanding." Stagnated beliefs become *concretized* and concrete cracks if walked on too long. Science also navigates uneven surfaces where past understandings are put to question. As I write, researchers from the CERN facility in Geneva, may have broken one of the most fundamental laws of physics, namely, exceeding the speed of light. They have recorded neutrinos (subatomic particles) traveling faster than the speed of light. If verified, this may cause the laws of physics to be re-written.

Newtonian physics characterized by: "cause and effect," "determinism," and the "whole comprises a certain number of parts" was virtually unassailable until Einstein formulated his relativity theories. And now we have "String Theory" whose proponents postulate "indeterminacy," which among other fantastic mathematical possibilities, suggests there are at least 11 dimensions; past, present, and future are co-existent perceptions; subatomic "entanglement" ("Beam me up, Scotty") may see us disassemble and reassemble our atoms to distant places; replicas of you and me may exist in alternative realities. "I had come for certitude," said Walter Brueggemann, "but the poetic speech does not give certitude."[70] Poetry, like scripture, illumines *and* obscures meaning even when a poet knows what he or she is striving to convey. I don't understand String Theory. My saving grace is *traditional physicists* deem String Theory a philosophy as opposed to science while theoretical physicists seek to unravel its mysteries. I celebrate String Theory's central thesis of "unification"—the conviction that the spiritual and temporal are undivided. Incarnation is not a third party exclusive event but first party experience and cosmic reality.

String Theory

Vibrating strings of energy unmeasured and unseen
  here, then there, then everywhere, no pathways in-between.
Like sightless, spinning dancers swirling into being
  multiverse realities are hidden from the scene.
Their microscopic overtures resounding day and night
  in rhythms, unpredictable, birthing death and life
  within, without, around, about wave-particles and light.
Creation's strange sweet symphony composes life's nativities
  beyond myopic sight.
Exploding probabilities unnumbered and untamed.
A throbbing twirling universe within each drop of rain.
Laws of relativity in quantum leaps reframed
Majestic spiral nebulae, atoms, protons, quarks.
The sum of every whole, far greater than its parts.
Side-by-side dimensions? Another you and me
  multiplied a million times in worlds we cannot see?
Physics or philosophy? Untested. Unexplained.
The fabric of the cosmos mysteriously contained
  in small and large infinities whose essence is the same.
Mindless probabilities or endless holy chants?
For deep within the pulse and play of creation's dance,
  time and space are strangely wed beyond mere whim and chance.
An abiding, "Deep Reality," plucks each and every string.
Amid discordant harmonies, all creation SINGS!

Reflection: Finding Level Ground

Someone said, "The ground is level at the foot of the cross." On this small, sacred, scrap of ground, no one stands above the other. Grace kisses diversity, equity swallows inequity, and the great unwashed are never washed away. Race, face, status, and place merge into one. Whether Christian, Jew, Muslim, Hindu, Buddhist, Sikh, Wiccan, agnostic or atheist, life's moral imperative strives to expand the arc of sacred footing to encompass the worth of all souls.

The Dance Partner

Never trust a religion that doesn't begin
*   and end in a doxology.*
And never trust a God who doesn't dance.
You do dance, don't you God? You said,
*   "We are that we might have joy!"*
And joy is in your dance—life's rhythmic smile
*   that grins in good times and bad.*
Not a sweet saccharine smile.
Not one of those mindless, high-voltage,
*   life-is-always-wonderful, smiles!*
Let's get real, God. Life's unfair!
Babies die, and innocent lives are swept away
*   by choice and circumstance.*

It's not that the dance doesn't get interrupted,
*   or that the music never stops.*
It does. And it's tempting to say,
"I can't dance to this tune—I'll sit this one out."
It's a matter of doing your best in the worst of times
*   —of stumbling through life's bumpy rhythms*
*   knowing you don't dance alone.*

Sad tears or glad tears—shadows live by sunlight.
Every night seeks a sunrise and every sunrise sings God's joy.
And so, I dance with a partner who never grows weary
*   of showing me new steps.*
And whenever I step on Yahwey's toes,
*   God shrugs, smiles, and joyfully dances on.*

167

Uneasy Morning

When time had no name, awareness sang no song
  —no why, how, where, or who, no mysteries to confound
  a mind asleep to all that is— 'till consciousness dispersed the fog
  and somehow god was born?
Nestled in the transitory. Springing from the shock:
  tomorrow begs no promise; breath has numbered days;
  the rising of the sun begets its setting
  and night shall claim us all.
The why, the how, the who, the angst of life's frail edges
  conceived by stark awakenings that something makes this so.

On this uneasy morning reflex dies, minds arise,
  fate echoes its refrain: The dawning of anxiety!
Transcendence on the rise! Within the womb of consciousness
  religion finds its home when trembling fears
  are put to rest with songs and sacrifice
  —to please the gods that spin strange webs
  of blessings now and then—to reap the promise, "Death is dead,"
  and just beyond its door, lie streets of gold, endless days,
  and feathered angel wings.
Houselights down, curtain up, Theism's Grand Début
  —rewards and retributions
  —a three-act play composed for me and you.
So, sleep soundly now. Fear no more—for god is birthed
  by ticking clocks wound by self-awareness
  —the stepchild of mortality that soars above the stars
  and stretches life for good or bad by choices that are ours
  . . . at least, that's how the story goes.

Where Does Faith Abide?

Where does faith abide—in miracles and mysteries,
  in power unsurpassed, in empty tombs, in parted seas,
  and prophecies forecast?
Is God a cosmic conjurer we court and seek to please
  with fingers crossed, petitions raised on sacramental knees?
When thousands die in raging winds, and two survive the storm
  are they loved more than all of those whose families will mourn?
Can might alone defeat the dark and turn the night to day

and where is God when loved ones cry and anguish has its way?
Are blessings scattered here and there with no address or home
    —a supernatural lottery of magic tricks alone?
Or are our tears the tears of God, and are our hopes God's own
    —are our prayers the prayers of God and not our pleas alone?
Omnipotence is not a friend when suffering
    wins the day and screams its name above the din
    of tearful prayers we pray to stay the hand of tragedy
    and keep death's sting at bay.
Surely One who plots the paths of swirling stars in space,
    who shapes a leaf, whose breath give lease
    to every shining face can bend the notes of nature's song
    for we who sing God's grace.
Yet, power alone cannot erase the choices that we make,
    the cause/effect of circumstance—the paths we choose to take.
A God who can do anything and chooses not to act
    is less than one whose hands are tied and weeps because He can't.
And when we place a premium on potency and might,
    we strip our God of empathy ignoring LOVE'S respite.
For LOVE cannot divorce itself from ecstasy and pain
    —the fire and ice that stirs life's tears and births new joy again.
Might alone is powerless to quell our trembling fear
    of living-bombs in lofty towers, of war's alarms,
    and sleepless hours when terrorism's near.
But 'terror' has no loyalty despite which flag is flown
    —the stars and stripes of 'Shock and Awe' are symbols that we own.
Missile strikes, and mushroom clouds are not the tools of peace
    for strength alone is powerless to grant our world release
    from martyrs of a tribal god whose vengeance will not cease.
Are we who sing God's majesty who pray for sun and rain,
    for winning games and parking spots much different or the same
    as they who pull the strings of God and do things in God's name?
Our battle hymns, fiery flames, unholy wars unending
    spill God's tears on blood-soaked ground incessant, unrelenting.
Who is chosen? Who is not? Who is blessed and who is not?
Are we God's or is God ours fashioned in our dreams
    —a grand design of deity unlimited, unleashed
    whose names we sign on drones and bombs
    that never seem to cease?

Silent Conversations

Your first word and last word
  and all those other words in between
  snuffed out by sweep second hands
  that give no quarter.
A lifetime of conversations.
Words of hope and attribution.
Words of reproof and anger.
Gentle whispers, smiles, and chuckles,
  Tears, and torment tucked away in phrases
  shared, and sometimes saved.
Twenty-six letters tumbling from tongue to ear
  bridging thoughts, stirring feelings
  filled with joy or fear.
What can be said that has not been said,
  carved in stone, or scribed by pen?
Endless wonderings. Nameless shades of night.
The sting of winter wind. Music fluttering the soul.
A wink, a look, a tender touch
  —the rush and blush of newfound love.

Words betray the poet—paint and stone, the artist.
Preachers pray for some new way to catch the light of God
  and let it shine in what they say
  in sermons preached, and scriptures taught.
And we who sing, and pray, and hear
  do not discern what lies between
  their first word and their last.
The soul they seek is but their own—
  a private convocation.
Unuttered cries that go unheard
  in search of benediction
  as deep within they probe doubt's night
  in silent conversations.

Servant of All
Joan Elaine Brown

Joan Brown epitomizes the central thrust of this volume as one who appeared ordinary but was anything but ordinary. Her "extraordinariness" shone brightly—free of fanfare and spotlights. It came naturally from within. Intelligent, kind, wise, and caring, Joan was perpetually sensitive to the needs of others. She was a past board member and treasurer for Independence Meals on Wheels and served Walnut Gardens congregation as a church school teacher, financial officer, building committee member, and counselor to the pastor among other roles, for forty years.

Joan's abiding flaw was her inability to realize the unique blessing she was to friend and stranger. She neither inflated her worth nor put herself down. Her humility reflected her natural desire to put the needs of others above her own. Her acceptance and love for others fueled their love for her. She would be embarrassed by this praise. Whatever failings besought her were overshadowed by her desire to share joy, hope, love, peace with others. Wife, mother, sister, grandmother, Christian witness, pastor, and friend, Joan passed away April 7, 2014. She is missed by all who knew her.

DAVID BROWN

"Many authors have attempted to help provide an understanding of love. They include unknown authors of sacred writings for various religions, authors of fiction that are now considered classic literature, poets whose words somehow speak simultaneously to intellect and heart, and lyricists who match words to music, so we can waft our way toward love. Yet, we struggle for a complete understanding of what love is and what love does. Joan was not an author of words for others to read. But she was an author on all with whom she came in contact, and her message was simple. Love is alive! It was alive in the smile that almost always graced her face. It was alive in her infectious laugh that was never derisive but always welcoming. It was alive in the effort she made to include everyone in whatever activity was taking place around her. It was alive in the quiet ministry she provided that acknowledged the presence of God in everyone she met. Though Joan's body now is described as dead, her love is still alive. It's alive in her children and grandchildren, who were closest to her aliveness. It's alive in everyone who was fortunate enough to be a tablet upon which she wrote. Her love is alive because she knew love does not exist just to exist. Love exists to support relationships, and relationships are what make us alive."

Dawning

Tell me, God, how many resurrections make a life? So many deaths to die: selfishness, cowardice, apathy, the hope for a hero's welcome. My daily struggle to kill the beast within: the hunger for words of praise, limelight's glow, and center-stage. Wind, surf, sand, and sea, the cosmos here to serve me. Each night I sleep through nothingness, inert—a mindless emptiness. The blessed death of selfishness—slain by silent midnight hours that promise no tomorrow till morning rolls the stone away with wispy dreams ascending. Each dawn's a new awakening. A day of resurrection. Alive to every soul I see. Alive to all I'm meant to be. Alive to One who grants to me a thousand Easter morns. Dismiss the night. Drink in the day! Hope dawns in you and me!

Her Abiding Presence

One heart-beat. One voice. One smile.
One face among the masses blurred and blending
*   her single note in the symphony of creation.*
Unique, unrepeated, she walked among us laughing, crying,
*   caring, sharing, giving and taking,*
*   making her way amid the music of our lives*
*   —adding to our song.*
A song now suddenly silent
*   heard only in the soft echoes of memory.*
Her face in faded photographs.
Her life cut short by death's sharp sting
*   —that great divide between here and there*
*   and what may be or may not be beyond life's composition.*
"Too soon!" we cry, "too soon before her time
*   —our time with her, her time with us*
And yet, her song sings on. Not by platitudes, scripture texts,
*   or saccharine sayings spun by wishful thinking.*
But, by a faithful knowing, an abiding presence
*   —an "imperative closeness"—that will not let us go!*
LOVE declares beyond reason's cold calculations
*   her melody with ours plays on, if we will but just listen.*

Reflection: Ego Inflation

Our priorities are misaligned. We are uncomfortable with the unknown, with anything that is not in some way measurable, containable and controllable. The cosmos "is" and in Barbara Brow Taylor's words, we are "devouring the creation whole and spitting out the seeds."[71] We have discovered formation's finger print and assume it just a matter of time before we shall grasp not only its finger but creation as a whole—all this amid a value system, which is remarkably uneven and skewed. A celebrity dies and a hundred million cry; a million die and no one cries." Like it or not, we are a people drunk on celebrity and individualism. In Western culture, particularly, the individual is deemed to be supreme. We pride ourselves in safeguarding individual rights and freedoms, as we should. But taken to its extreme, *preoccupation* with unbridled "ego-inflation" renders us a cult of celebrity where the priority of certain individuals rise above the collective. We rail against government health care programs because everyone should pull himself or herself up by their own bootstraps? God forbid we should share the cost of those who cannot. We proclaim each person is of equal worth, while in praxis some are worth more than others—pathologically satisfying our hunger for vicarious fame and importance.

There too, Go I

There too, go I, filled with hopes and dreams
  fraught by stumbling blocks and schemes
    that halt my starry climb
    to be who I must be.
Creation births each sacred child
  —thin, stout, short, tall
    shaped by Heaven's hands.
Nor are we shaped in vain,
  this blend of chromosomes and genes
  uniquely spun by stardust's strange sweet rhapsody.
A universe of highs and lows, of give and take.
God's endless possibilities
  unfolding for Love's sake
    with none deemed less or more.
There too, go I, one voice to speak for those who cannot speak,
  to stand for those cannot stand
  whose essence cries for equity,
  whose tears are pillow stained.
I see you, and you, see me.
Unique and yet the same,
  for I AM you and you ARE me.
The fingerprints of grace
  have left no soul untouched.

Reflection: "All About ME!"

"It's not all about YOU!" she shouted, reminding me the sun doesn't rise and set for my benefit. It doesn't of course, or does it? It's so easy to be the hub of existence, because that's where I am. Everything happens around me. *I AM the physical center of all I experience.* It's simply unavoidable. It's just the way things are. Look, "It's Not all About Me!" is a good phrase—a good dose of verbal humility—a good T-shirt slogan. However, paradoxically, it can't be ALL about me *without it being about YOU!* When I push ahead in line, put others down, expect a bigger piece of life's pie, it's also about you. When I make myself the moral center of the universe; when a helping hand is not extended; when I pass by on the other side; when I fail to speak for those cannot speak, stand for those who cannot stand, act for those who cannot act—it is about me, and *all about you.* Whenever I play it safe and sit on the sidelines it's all about me and you, because I am you and you are me. We are many. We are one. If it's about you; it IS about me!

One final poem of promise
in memory of **Joan Brown**,
pastor, servant, friend, wife
who brought joy, hope, love, and peace to her congregation;
her husband, Dave; her children; grandchildren; church family;
and all privileged to know her.

Promise Yourself

Promise yourself to laugh today, to let joy take your breath way
    wrapped up in simple things today
    —a cup of soup, a note, a card, a phone call to a friend.
Promise yourself to LOVE today, to let joy sweep the hurt away
    from wounding words that come your way
    and share instead a listening ear, a moment's grace, a smiling face.
Promise yourself to PAUSE today, to let joy have its way
    amid life's hurried swish and sway that snuff the sparks of ecstasy
    and drown the soul's sweet fantasies.
Promise yourself to FORGET today, to let joy purge your memories
    of hopes undone and songs unsung,
    of battles fought and nearly won.
Promise yourself to BE KIND today, to let joy flood your soul today
    with little deeds that plant love's seeds
    in young and old who pass your way.
Promise yourself to BREATHE today, to see, to hear, and feel this day,
    each vibrant note of joy today
    —a bird on the wing, a face in a cloud,
    a laugh, a chuckle, a child in the crowd.
Promise yourself to SING today,
    sweet symphonies of grace this day
    wrapped up in simple things.

Afterward

"Being religious means asking passionately the question of the meaning of our existence and being willing to receive answers, even if the answers hurt." —Paul Tillich[72]

"There can be no vulnerability without risk; there can be no community without vulnerability; there can be no peace, and ultimately no life, without community."—M. Scott Peck[73]

Community of Christ is my religious home and community. Because I served as a general officer, some readers may question whether my theology fits this denomination. My response is a resounding, "YES!" Community of Christ's concept of community is a circle without a circumference. All are welcome. The church's website states its mission is to *"Proclaim Jesus Christ and create communities of joy, love, and peace."* The website also describes the church's Basic Beliefs, paralleling mainline Christians tenants reflected in the ancient creeds. I consider the creeds seriously, but not literally. They have powerful symbolic meaning but are not a test of faith or Christian fellowship. Community of Christ does not mandate adherence to lockstep fixed theological declarations but encourages members and friends to pursue their unique understanding of Jesus and the discipleship to which he calls them.

The Christian creeds took place in church councils amid raucous debates, bitterness, and political compromise. Sadly, some seminary-trained ministers become party to a "conspiracy of silence'" by failing to engage parishioners with controversial issues and insights encountered in academia and commonplace among scholars. Truth should never be deterred just because it is inconvenient or disquieting. While we must guard against acrimony in attempts to articulate our faith, we are obligated to engage in a process wherein we mutually listen with respect, ask with intent, speak with courage, and seek to discern the whisper of truth's spirit guiding us.

The gospel or "good news" is the right arrangement of relationships. It is not a set of impregnable declarations or salvific rituals. The gospel is incarnated whenever our eyes, ears, hands, feet, and voice tangibly contribute to creation's highest good. It is incarnated when we awaken to life's wonder and live it, when belief becomes biography, and when dualism no longer divides the sacred from the secular. Progressive Christian minister, Michael Dowd, offers the following challenging mission statement.

There are many different world views that inspire people to live in right relationship to reality. The one I'm particularly passionate about I've come to call the path of sacred realism or factual faith. I'm an evidential mystic. Reality is my God, and evidence is my scripture. Big history is my creation story, and ecology is my theology. Integrity is my salvation, and ensuring a just and healthy future, not just for humanity but for the entire body of life, is my mission.[74]

The cosmos is real. You are real. I am real. We are not self-existent, external observers; we are entities within a living universe. Said another way, we *are* the earth, sea, sand, soil, the grass beneath our feet, flame, fury, raging wind, calming breeze, the hush of night. We are integral to creation's strange evolving dance—a sacred confluence of "cosmological community," birthing what has been, what is, and what shall be. *"Uni-verse"* means "one" realty. *Reality* is God's loudest witness.

Two and a half millennia before Emmanuel Kant declared, "I think therefor I am," the author(s) of Exodus put God's name on Moses's lips, "I am that I am." The strongest argument for God's existence is not philosophical or theological, but existence itself. Reality is stamped with God's fingerprints. The term *community,* whether applied to life's convergence of atoms, the birth of stars and planets, or a warm handshake of acceptance and support is divinity's reality. We are our brother's, sister's, and ecology's keeper. Nothing is an "it"; everything is a "thou." Kyaw Thu, Burmese film actor and director, echoes life's mutual belongingness with these words, *"The people's tears are your tears. The people's happiness is your happiness."*[75] You and I contribute to life's emerging possibilities. *Goodness is paid forward!* One single act of kindness blesses untold others.

Somewhere a small child said, "I want to be just like you!"
And it's making all the difference in the world.
Somewhere, a young man or lady is attending college, or beginning a new
job, moving to a new town, or taking on a new challenge and is hoping to
become just like you! And it's making all the difference in world.
Somewhere, someone is reading something you wrote, quoting something you
said, remembering some gift left behind, laughing with joy at
something you said or did. And it's making all the difference in the world.
Somewhere, you helped someone say, "No!" when "no" needed saying, and
"Yes!" when courage teetered in the balance.
Somewhere, you took someone's hand, looked pain in the face, listened
intently, never uttered a word, and it made all the difference in the world.
Somewhere, there is a name you never heard, a hand you never shook, a face
you never noticed who caught a piece of hope you tossed along the way,
and it has made all the difference in the world.
Somewhere a long time ago, "Someone" called your name down deep in the
recesses of your soul, and it has made all the difference in the world.
And somewhere, "Someone or Something" is reminding you that a shared cup of
coffee, a friendly handshake, a card, a pat on the back, a brief phone call, a
wave, a look, and a smile can make all the difference.
Someone or something needs your voice, your touch,
your listening ear, and helping hand.
Someone or something is saying, "You can make all the difference in the world.
Look at all these 'ordinary people' living extraordinary lives!"

About the Author

Danny A. Belrose is an ordained minister, amateur poet, and artist. He attended Saint Paul School of Theology, Kansas City, Missouri, and St. Stephen's College in Edmonton, Alberta, Canada, where he graduated with a master of theology and doctor of ministry degree. Dr. Belrose is the author of *Let the Spirit Breathe*, *Wave Offerings*, *Vulnerable to Grace* and several hymn texts in *Community of Christ Sings* published in 2013.

Danny and his wife, Penelope Lynne (Prior) Belrose, are dual US/Canadian citizens and reside in Independence, Missouri. They are parents to three daughters, Beth Ann Morden (deceased), Kerry Lee Peters, and Heather Lynn Moor. Before retirement, Danny served as a general officer of Community of Christ's International Headquarters and ministered in several countries. He describes himself as a liberal, process oriented, Christian:

Nouns endure. Adjectives are transitory; they merely describe the lens through which I presently perceive my Christian faith. Certitude begs no epiphanies, no hills to climb, no higher hopes. I have learned to say, "It seems to me" rather than "That's the way it is!" because theology's articulation of life's deeper reality is forever wanting.

Theology comes down to poetry—the language of symbolism. Religious beliefs are propositions; we sing them; say them; preach them; pray them and thank God we change them. Conversely, religious faith is "in-vocational." Faith is not couched in declarative statements, but is a persistent call to invest relentless hope in God's present and future. A good friend, JW Windland, said, "There is a difference between believing Jesus and believing in Jesus." I believe Jesus. I believe Jesus demonstrated what it means to be fully human and fully divine, just as you and I are human and divine. Incarnation is not an exclusive third-party event, but a first party and cosmic reality.

Though I consider the ancient Christian creeds symbolic rather than literal, I am a committed disciple of Jesus. Definitions and adjectives come and go but the nouns "disciple" and "Christian" tug at me daily because that is whom I am attempting to be.

Danny is the author of *Let the Spirit Breathe*, *Wave Offerings*, *Vulnerable to Grace*, and several hymn texts in *Community of Christ Sings* published under *Herald Publishing House* imprint.

[1] C. S. Lewis, *The Weight of Glory: And Other Addresses* (HarperCollins e-books) Downloaded from Amazon.com, 46–47, Location 431–432.

[2] Walter Brueggemann, *Finally Comes the Poet: Daring Speech for Proclamation* (Minneapolis: Fortress Press, 1989), 2.

[3] Joseph Campbell echoes C.S. Lewis's perspective re ordinary people: "I always feel uncomfortable when people speak about 'ordinary mortals' because I've never met an ordinary man, woman, or child." Joseph Campbell, *The Power of Myth with Bill Moyers*, Ed. Betty Sue Flowers (New York: Double Day, 1988), 163.

[4] J. W. Windland, comparative mythologist and founder of Canada's Encounter World Religions Centre in an unpublished paper *"Christian Mission in a Multifaith World"* writes: "It seems to me that shifting the business of the church from 'salvation to a heavenly realm' to 'salvation from present suffering' is a shift from ideology to action, is a shift from a message about an incarnation to a message incarnate, is a shift from 'belief in Jesus,' which requires intellectual assent to 'believing Jesus,' which requires risk and vulnerability."

[5] Danny A. Belrose, *Let the Spirit Breathe* (Independence, MO: Herald Publishing House, 2004), 93.

[6] Harry Emerson Fosdick, *Dear Mr. Brown: Letters to a Person Perplexed About Religion* (New York: Harper & Brothers, 1961) Quote downloaded from https://www.azquotes.com/quote/1269281" title="Harry Emerson Fosdick quote"><img src="//www.azquotes.com/

[7] Campbell, *The Power of Myth,* 49.

[8] Frederick Buechner, *The Alphabet of Grace* (HarperCollins e-book, copyright 1970) 49, Location 524 of 2,527.

[9] C. S. Lewis. *Surprised by Joy: The Shape of My Early Life*, (San Francisco: HarperOne, 2017).

[10] Joseph Campbell posits, "Eternity isn't some later time. Eternity isn't a long time. Eternity has nothing to do with time. Eternity is that dimension of here and now which thinking and time cuts out. This is it. And if you don't get it here, you won't get it anywhere. And the experience of eternity right here and now is the function of life."—Campbell, *The Power of Myth,* 67.

[11] "Mr. Potato Head," was invented and developed by George Lerner in 1949, and first manufactured and distributed by Hasbro in 1952.

[12] Sophia is found throughout the wisdom books of the Bible. The following is from Eric Edwards Collected Works— *"The Cult of the Mother Goddess: 1) Antecedents of the Goddess Cult:* "The idea of the goddess as mother can

be found with the prehistoric ancestors of modern humans. Some 30,000 years ago early religion, which was a feature of human evolution." https://www.ericwedwards.wordpress.com/2013/07/17/the-cult-of-the-mother-goddess/

[13] Campbell, *The Power of Myth,* 14.

[14] "The least, the lost, the labeled" attributed to Stephen M. Veazey, president of Community or Christ.

[15] According to the online encyclopedia, Wikipedia, all 13 tracks of the rock band the Beatles' *"A Hard Day's Night"* album (released 10 July 1964) were written by John Lennon and Paul McCartney. Title of the album is attributed to Richard Starkey (Ringo Star). See https://en.wikipedia.org/wiki/A_Hard_-Day%27s_Night_(album). The Wikipedia page was last edited 22 July 2018, at 13:52 (UTC).

[16] The "Roy Rogers" movie serial does not reference an actual film.

[17] The phrases "too muchness" and "too littleness" attributed to Frederick Buechner, *The Sacred Journey: A Memoir of Early Days* (San Francisco: Harper, 1982), pp. 102–104.

[18] Adapted from https://www.en.wikipedia.org/wiki/The_Friendly_Giant. This page was last edited 11 July 2018, at 03:27 (UTC).

[19] The phrase, "When the lights go out and life tumbles in" was published in "The Elwood Call-Leader," Saturday, April 7, 1962. (https://www.newspapers.com/newspage/87902153).

[20] Bertrand Russell, *Why Men Fight: A Method of Abolishing the International Duel* (New York: The Century Company, 1917), e-book, location,1,532.

[21] Danny Belrose, *Vulnerable to Grace: A Study and Worship Resource Exploring Section 163* (Independence, MO: Herald Publishing House, 2008), 106.

[22] Danny Belrose, *Wave Offerings: Personal Psalms, Prayers, and Pieces* (Herald Publishing House, Independence, MO., 2005), 30.

[23] The phrase, *"Friendship multiplies joys and divides griefs"* attributed to Thomas Fuller, seventeenth century English churchman and historian.

[24] White & Case Internet profile of Debashis Dey. https://www.whitecase.com/people/debashis-dey.

[25] Belrose. *Vulnerable to Grace,* 95.

[26] Wallace Stevens, poem "Sunday Morning" published in part in the November 1915 issue of *Poetry*, then in full in 1923 in *Harmonium*, is now in the public domain.

[27] Jean-Pierre de Caussade's, *The Sacrament of the Present Moment* is a three hundred year-old classic of spiritual guidance and enlightenment.

[28] Melissa Hung. *"Meet the 70-Year Old Runner Who Ran 7 Marathons on 7 Continents in 7 Days"* (https://www.nbcnews.com/news/asian-america/

meet-70-year-old-runner-who-ran-7-marathons-7-n722551).

[29] Terry Young, "Local Woman Brings Family to US" (*The Independence Examiner*, Blue Springs, Vol 21, No 98 and Independence, Vol. 90, No 103) December 24–25, 1994, Front Page, continued on page 7A.

[30] See online encyclopedia Wikipedia, "Theodicy" https://en.wikipedia.org/wiki/Theodicy. This page was last edited 24 June 2018, at 13:12 (UTC).

[31] Choan-Seng Song, *The Compassionate God* (Markknoll, N.Y.: Orbis, 1981), 109.

[32] Mainly in response to the issue of theodicy, a number of theologians reject God's omnipotence. Bishop John Shelby Spong states, "The theistic God was a being like us human beings in all details, except with human limitations removed. We called God infinite and immortal because we knew ourselves to be finite and mortal. We called God omnipotent and omnipresent because we knew human life to be powerless and ultimately bound by space. We called God omniscient because we knew ourselves to be limited in knowledge. Only a deity not bound by our weaknesses could address the anxieties of our limits and provide us with the security we sought. Then we named this deity "Father" or "Almighty Father,"—John Shelby Spong, *Unbelievable: Why Neither Ancient Creeds Nor the Reformation Can Produce a Living Faith Today* (HarperCollins, Kindle e-book) 51–52.

[33] Douglas John Hall, *God and Human Suffering: An Exercise in the Theology of the Cross* (Minneapolis: Augsburg Publishing House, 1986), 67–70.

[34] Popularly attributed to Einstein.

[35] Some researchers suggest this quote is not attributed to Einstein but to Alexander Pope, the 18th Century English poet, from his "Essay on Criticism" (written in 1709 and published in 1711, Pope wrote: "A little Learning is a dang'rous Thing; Drink deep, or taste not the Pierian [peer-ee-an] Spring: There shallow Draughts intoxicate the Brain, And drinking largely sobers us again."

[36] Danny Belrose, *By Request: Songs for the Community of Christ* (ISBN 0-8309-1108-1, Community of Christ Copyright Corporation, Independence, MO. 2004), R-6.

[37] "Alphabet of grace," attributed to Frederick Buechner.

[38] Video lecture by Bishop John Shelby Spong: *"Who is the popular God in Public Life in the 21st Century"* delivered at the University of Oregon, https://youtu.be/PwNmj5h1zds?t=585.

[39] Belrose, *Vulnerable to Grace,* 35.

[40] Ibid., 36.

[41] Ibid., 103.

[42] Nelle Morton, from her 1977 essay "Beloved Image," reprinted in the book *The Journey is Home.* Quote downloaded from http://actsofhope.blogspot.com/2007/08/hearing-to-speech.html. Posted by Jane Redmont, Tuesday,

August 21, 2007.

[43] Belrose, *Vulnerable to Grace,* 109.

[44] Ibid., 44.

[45] Emily Dickenson, *The Poems of Emily Dickenson Reading Edition* (Belknap Press of Harvest University Press 1998), Selection, "Tell all the truth but tell it slant."

[46] *Community of Christ Sings* (Herald Publishing House, 2013) hymn 69, "We Limit Not the Truth of God."

[47] Rohr, Richard Rohr, *"Going to the Depth of the Manager"* video series, 2226305, www.theworkofthepeople.com.

[48] "Seek for truth; come. Whence it may, lead where it will, cost what it may" attributed to William Sparrow, 1801—1874, Professor of Theology and dean of *Virginia Theological Seminary*. His statement is inscribed on his gravestone and at the entrance to the seminary's library in Virginia.

[49] Belrose, *Vulnerable to Grace*, 21.

[50] Ibid., 45.

[51] Ibid., 97.

[52] As quoted by Gregg Braden, *The Isaiah Effect* (New York: Three Rivers Press, 2000), 44.

[53] Ibid., 88.

[54] Johnnie Taylor, "T*oo Much Week at The End of The Money,"* (Real Love album, release date: February 14, 1994).

[55] Ibid., 46.

[56] Belrose, *"Wave Offerings,* 141.

[57] Belrose, *Vulnerable to Grace,* 71.

[58] Kate Chiles Graham, "Reaching the Place," *National Catholic Reporter: The Independent News Source.* Blog, Dec. 15, 2011.

[59] The phrase, "hemorrhaging of the soul" is not original. I have been unsuccessful in attributing its derivation. The earliest source may be Jean Paul Sartre' statement: "Shame is the hemorrhage of the soul."

[60] Belrose, *Vulnerable to Grace,* "Acknowledgments," 6.

[61] Frederick Greeves, *Forgiveness and Reconciliation* (Macmillan 1941), 13–14,

[62] Leslie D. Weatherhead, *The Christian Agnostic*, (Abingdon Press, Nashville, 1965), 29.

[63] Marjorie Hewitt Suchocki referencing John Cobb in *Divinity & Diversity: A Christian Affirmation of Religious Pluralism* (Nashville, Abingdon Press, 2003), 20-21.

[64] Ibid., 49, Location 441.

[65] Robert Galbraith, a.k.a. J. K. Rowling, *The Cuckoo's Calling* (New York, NY, Mulholland Books/ Little Brown and Company, Hachette Book Group, e-book 2013), location 550 of 6,708.

[66] The lyric, "The fourth, the fifth, the minor fall, the major lift" attributed to Leonard Cohen's classic composition, *"Hallelujah"* recorded at Quadrasonic Sound, New. York, 11 December 1984.

[67] William Cleary, *Prayers to an Evolutionary God* (Woodstock Vermont: Skylight Paths Publishing, 2004). 120.

[68] Einstein's essay, "Science and Religion," published in 1954.

[69] Pierre Teilhard de Chardin, *The Phenomenon of Man* (New York: Harper and Row, 1961), 283.

[70] Walter Brueggemann, *Finally Comes The Poet: Daring Speech For Proclamation,* (Minneapolis: Fortress Press, 1989), 10.

[71] Barbara Brown Taylor, *The Preaching Life,* (New York, NY: A Cowley Publication Book, Rowman & Littlefield Publishers, Inc. Kindle Edition) 40, location 604.

[72] F. Forrester Church, *The Essential Tillich: An Anthology of The Writings of Paul Tillich* (New York, NY: Macmillan Publishing Company, 1987), 1.

[73] M. Scott Peck, *The Different Drum: Community-Making and Peace* (Simon & Schuster, 1987). Quote downloaded: http://thinkexist.com/quotation/there_can_be_no_vulnerability_without_risk-there/339057.html.

[74] Michael Dowd, *"My TedX Talk: Reality Reconciles Science and Religion."* Quote downloaded from Huddpost Website, updated August 20, 2014. https://www.huffingtonpost.com/rev-michael-dowd/tedx-talk-reality-reconci_b_5513264.html.

[75] Amina Rasul quotes Kyaw Thu in her article, *"Unleashing The Power of Ordinary Citizens,"* posted and published Monday 27, September 2015, 0:36, on the "Institute For Autonomy and Governance: Sharing Public Policy for Peace and Good Governance" website: https://iag.org.ph/index.php/blog/1209-unleashing-the-power-of-ordinary-citizens.

Made in the USA
Columbia, SC
25 March 2019